Dec /96

To Adam,

Best wishes!

A Declaration of Taxpayer Rights

BATEMAN MACKAY
CHARTERED ACCOUNTANTS

Author
Timothy J. Cestnick, B. Comm., C.A.

Editor
Gary L. Bateman, P. Eng., M.B.A., C.A.

Contributions
David C. Sabina, M.B.A., C.A.

PUBLISHED BY
BATEMAN FINANCIAL CONSULTANTS LIMITED

Canadian Cataloguing in Publication Data

Cestnick, Timothy J., 1966-
    A declaration of taxpayer rights

Includes index.
ISBN 0-9680395-0-2

        1. Tax planning—Canada—Popular works.
2. Income tax—Canada. I. Bateman, Gary, 1947-
II. Bateman Financial Consultants. III. Title.
IV. Title: Taxpayer rights.

HJ4661.C48 1996   343.7105'2   C95-920822-4

How to get additional copies of this book:

1. See your local bookstore
2. Contact the publisher at:

Bateman Financial Consultants Limited
3410 South Service Road, P.O. Box 5015
Burlington, Ontario L7R 3Y8

Phone: (905) 632-6400
Fax: (905) 639-2285
http://www.bateman-mackay.com
email: bateman@bateman-mackay.com

Printed in Canada by Eagle Press, Burlington, Ontario

Cover photo: Tony Stone Images

About Our Firm

Bateman MacKay is an income tax focused firm of Chartered Accountants located in Burlington, Ontario. Our firm combines uniquely specialized individuals committed to high quality, personalized, tax-oriented service for a variety of individuals and companies - while maintaining our sense of humour.

Timothy J. Cestnick, B.Comm., C.A.

Tim is a graduate of the University of Toronto. Following university he obtained his C.A. designation and then completed the CICA's In-Depth Tax Course and the Canadian Securities Course. He is experienced in all areas of personal income taxation, particularly related to owner-managers, and U.S. personal tax. Tim has authored numerous tax articles in a variety of publications, has appeared on television, and is the author of this book.

Gary L. Bateman, P.Eng., M.B.A., C.A.

Gary is the founder of our firm. He has taught taxation at the CICA's In-Depth Tax Course, McMaster University, and for the Ontario Institute of Chartered Accountants. In addition to authoring the *Guide to the Taxation of R&D Expenses* published by Carswell, Gary is a member of the Estate Planner's Council of Toronto, has appeared on television, and is an authority in Canada on Research and Development tax incentives.

David C. Sabina, M.B.A., C.A.

After graduating from York University, David obtained his C.A. designation and his M.B.A., then completed the CICA's In-Depth Tax Course and the Canadian Securities Course. He has taught tax courses for the Ontario Institute of Chartered Accountants and various other organizations. David is also a contributor to the *Guide to the Taxation of R&D Expenses*, and co-author of the CICA interactive software learning program *The Taxation of Scientific Research and Experimental Development Expenses.*

Dedication

This book is dedicated to Canadian taxpayers everywhere who, despite their best efforts, are paying more in taxes than they have a right to pay; and to our clients who, through their own questions and circumstances, have given us the opportunity and desire to research the material for this book.

Disclaimer

The information and ideas contained in this book are not intended to substitute for professional tax advice since such advice should be tailored to suit your specific circumstances. This book is intended as a general guide to bring to your attention opportunities available for minimizing your taxes. Consult your tax professional before implementing any tax strategies with which you are not completely familiar or comfortable.

Overview

Page

Foreword

Chapter 1   The Right To Pay Less Tax   1
Chapter 2   Laying The Foundation   5

PART I: THE PILLARS OF TAX PLANNING
Chapter 3   Reducing Taxable Income   17
Chapter 4   Splitting Taxable Income   45
Chapter 5   Deferring Taxable Income   61
Chapter 6   Converting Taxable Income   77

PART II: SPECIAL AREAS
Chapter 7   Getting The Most From Your RRSP   93
Chapter 8   Self-Employment   147

PART III: INVESTING YOUR MONEY
Chapter 9   Investment Basics   173
Chapter 10   Where To Put Your Money   187

Last Word   212

Appendices   213

Index   225

What's Inside

	Lesson	Page
Foreword		
1. The Right To Pay Less Tax		
2. Laying The Foundation		
Tax evasion and avoidance	1	5
Marginal and effective tax rates	2	6
Tax deductions vs. credits	3	8
A dollar today vs. a dollar tomorrow	4	9
The five rules of thumb	5	10
Understanding GAAR	6	12
Finding professional tax advice	7	13

PART I: THE PILLARS OF TAX PLANNING

3. Reducing Taxable Income	Lesson	Page
DEDUCTIONS AGAINST INCOME		
Deductions for employees	8	19
Deducting RRSP contributions	9	21
Interest and carrying charges	10	22
Moving expenses	11	23
Child care expenses	12	24
Allowable business investment losses	13	26
Employee stock options	14	26
Stock appreciation rights	15	28
Capital gains exemption - still here	16	29
Triggering capital losses	17	30
Mutual fund distributions	18	31
Gains and losses: income vs. capital	19	32
Business and professional losses	20	34
Limited partnerships	21	35
When you forget a deduction	22	36

NON-TAXABLE BENEFITS
Non-taxable benefits   23   36
Death benefits   24   41

TAXABLE BENEFITS
Taxable benefits   25   41
Employee loans   26   42

4.   Splitting Taxable Income

Making use of loans   27   46
Transferring property   28   49
Giving away deductions and credits   29   52
Investing cash in the right hands   30   54
Using statutory provisions   31   56
Using a business or corporation   32   57

5.   Deferring Taxable Income

Tax-deferred plans   33   62
The timing of investment income   34   68
Using a business or corporation   35   71

6.   Converting Taxable Income

WHAT IS CONVERSION?
Interest, dividends, and capital gains   36   78
Converting interest to dividends   37   78
Capital gains exemption   38   79
Depending on interest   39   80
Investment amnesia   40   81

HOW TO CONVERT TAXABLE INCOME
Equity mutual funds   41   82
Common and preferred shares   42   82
Swapping investments with your RRSP   43   83
Your principal residence   44   84
Converting a loan to share capital   45   85
Exempt life insurance policies   46   86

Annuities: non-taxable?	47	87
When you sell capital property	48	88

PART II: SPECIAL AREAS

7. Getting The Most From Your RRSP

AN INTRODUCTION TO RRSPs
What is an RRSP?	49	93
Advantages of an RRSP	50	94
RRSPs and your creditors	51	96
Administration fees	52	97

CONTRIBUTING TO YOUR RRSP
Contribution limits	53	98
Increasing your contribution limits	54	100
Your child's contributions	55	100
Starting RRSP contributions	56	101
When to contribute each year	57	102
Unused contribution room	58	104
Borrowing to contribute	59	104
Over-contributing	60	106
Claiming your deduction at the right time	61	106
RRSP vs. your mortgage	62	107
Contributions in-kind	63	109

SPECIAL ROLLOVERS
Retiring and termination allowances	64	110
Registered Pension Plans	65	111
U.S.A. Individual Retirement Accounts	66	114
RRSPs inherited	67	114
Transfers to another RRSP	68	116
Transfers upon marriage break-up	69	117

SPOUSAL RRSPs
What is a spousal RRSP?	70	117
Which spouse should contribute?	71	118
Attribution on withdrawals	72	119
When to contribute each year	73	120

Contributing after age 71   74   121
Contributing using a deceased's assets   75   122

SELF-DIRECTED RRSPs
What a self-directed RRSP is and when
to open one   76   123

INVESTING INSIDE YOUR RRSP
Non-qualified investments   77   124
Foreign content   78   125
Interest-bearing investments   79   128
Equity investments   80   128
Insurance protection for your RRSP   81   129

GETTING MONEY OUT OF YOUR RRSP
Getting money out when you retire
    Your three options   82   130
    Using the pension credit   83   132
Getting money out for a home purchase   84   134
Getting money out for personal use
    Periods of no or low income   85   137
    Withdrawing in increments   86   138
    Investing in your own mortgage   87   139
Getting money out when leaving Canada   88   141

8.   Self-Employment

BECOMING SELF-EMPLOYED
Self-employment as a tax shelter   89   148
Consulting   90   149
Part-time self-employment   91   151

YOUR BUSINESS: SAVING YOU TAXES
Capital cost allowance   92   152
Home office expenses   93   153
Automobile expenses   94   155
Meals and entertainment   95   156
Paying family members a salary   96   156
Paying for personal vs. business assets   97   157

Using losses from your business   98   158
Investment tax credits   99   160

STRUCTURING YOUR BUSINESS
The three structures to choose from   100   162
Choosing a year end   101   164

PAYMENTS TO THE TAXMAN
Unemployment insurance   102   166
Canada pension plan   103   166
Provincial payroll taxes   104   167
Tax instalments   105   168

PART III: INVESTING YOUR MONEY

9.   Investment Basics

RISK AND RETURN
The three investment classes   106   174
Different types of risk   107   175
Determining your risk tolerance   108   176

HOW TO INVEST
Strategic investing and market timing   109   178
Diversifying your portfolio   110   180
Diversifying internationally   111   181
Understanding and selecting investments 112   182

YOUR INVESTMENT ADVISOR
Choosing the right advisor   113   183
Different advisors for different needs 114   184
Minimizing commissions and fees   115   186

10.   Where to Put Your Money

Mutual funds: timing a purchase   116   187
Mutual funds: exempt capital gains   117   190
Limited partnerships   118   191
Labour-sponsored venture capital funds 119   195

Dividend reinvestment plans   120   197
Tax-deferred preferred shares   121   198
Offshore investing   122   200
Back to back prescribed annuities   123   203
Back to back with equity mutual funds   124   205
Exempt insurance policies   125   206
Commodity straddles   126   208
Canadian controlled private corporations   127   210

Last Word   212

Appendices

A declaration of taxpayer rights   1   215
Combined marginal tax rates   2   216
Federal personal tax rates   3   218
Provincial personal tax rates   4   219
Combined personal tax credits   5   221
Minimum annual RRIF withdrawals   6   223
Common capital cost allowance rates   7   224

Index   225

Foreword

I was sound asleep at work when I was startled by a crash. What would so rudely wake me? It was my Income Tax Act landing on the floor. I had been reading Section 80.01 when, surprisingly, I fell asleep. Trouble sleeping? Buy a copy of the Act.

I'm telling you this story so that you'll appreciate what I've been up against in writing this book. Writing a tax planning book that will not only educate but keep you awake in the process is no easy task. And I wanted this book to be different - I wanted it to be creative, easy to read and understand, easy to look at, as well as reliable. I think the final product accomplishes these things, and this is why the book is worth reading - I hope you'll agree.

Why did I write the book? For two reasons. First, I've authored articles before, and I love writing. Earning a living at what I enjoy makes me especially fortunate and thankful. Second, and most importantly, I wanted to provide you, the Canadian taxpayer, with the know-how to create a better life for yourself by paying less in taxes and keeping more in your pockets. A side benefit is that the book will be a valuable tool when solving clients' problems, teaching courses, and giving seminars.

I'm now convinced that an author always needs help. There's a long list of people whose efforts made this book possible, and they deserve my thanks. They include my friends in the investment industry, insurance industry, graphic design industry, and a lawyer or two. Thanks to my co-workers for their help and contributions, and to Gary Bateman, whose creativity and willingness to edit and publish this book made the whole thing possible.

Tim J. Cestnick
January 1996

The Right To Pay Less Tax

1

If one thing can be said about Canadians, it's that we're thoroughly taxed. So much for the income tax being a temporary measure! That's right, back in 1917 the government introduced the Income War Tax Act, levying a 4% tax on income (to help finance World War I) which many believed, based on comments made by Sir Thomas White, the Finance Minister of the day, to be a temporary tax. Someone should let Ottawa know that the war is over, because that 4% tax has increased to over 50% for many of us. Across the country, we've made it clear to the federal and provincial governments that we won't tolerate additional tax increases. Unfortunately, when it comes time to pay the taxman, many Canadians are not doing themselves any favours. Canadian taxpayers have certain rights as set out in the government's Declaration of Taxpayer Rights. You're entitled to know your rights and to insist that they be respected.

Your Most Important Right
The most important right that Canadian taxpayers are entitled to, and one that many people fail to exercise, is the right to arrange your affairs so as to pay the least amount of tax that the law will allow.

This was best expressed by Lord Tomlin in perhaps the most significant case in the history of tax planning, "I.R.C. vs. Duke of Westminster" (1936):

"Every man is entitled, if he can, to order his affairs so that the tax attaching under the appropriate Acts is less than it otherwise would be."

The purpose of this book is to help you exercise this right by guiding you through some creative and thoroughly legal ways to reduce your tax bill. Incidentally, reducing your taxes is not for the wealthy alone – it's possible at all income levels.

There are four general methods available to reduce your taxes. We call these *the four pillars of tax planning*. Any action you take to minimize your taxes will fall under one or more of these pillars.

The four pillars of tax planning:

- ### Reducing taxable income
- ### Splitting taxable income
- ### Deferring taxable income
- ### Converting taxable income

A chapter is devoted to each of these pillars in Part I of this book, and understanding them will equip you with the tools you'll need to minimize your taxes. You'll be introduced to some creative ideas in Part I, many of which our clients have used to minimize their own taxes.

In Part II of the book we'll look at two special areas where tax breaks are available to all Canadians: RRSPs and full or part-time self-employment. Keep in mind that in each of these special areas, where you're reducing your tax bill, one or more of the tax pillars will be present.

Part III of the book will focus on investing. We'll provide you with the know-how to ensure that you're maximizing your after-tax returns on your investments. After all, after-tax returns are the only kind you can spend. Your investments will be reviewed in light of the four pillars, which should further help you to understand them. In addition, you'll be introduced to some investment vocabulary which should help you to understand (and appear more knowledgeable to) your investment advisor.

By the way, there are certain other rights that you have as a Canadian taxpayer, and we firmly believe you should be aware of

them. In particular, you have the following rights in your dealings with Revenue Canada (see Appendix 1 at the back):
- the right to information
- the right to courtesy and consideration
- the right to impartiality
- the right to be presumed honest
- the right to privacy and confidentiality
- the right to withhold disputed amounts
- the right to an impartial review
- the right to bilingual service

This is a book for all Canadians. Whether your income is modest or substantial, from the shores of Newfoundland to the mountains of British Columbia, you have the right to pay less tax, and this book is the place to start.

Laying the Foundation

There are certain basics that every taxpayer should understand. In this chapter we introduce some of the more important things to you. These are valuable concepts, and throughout the book we'll be referring to things like your marginal tax rate, effective tax rate, deductions, credits, and more, so laying the foundation here with a brief discussion makes good sense. Don't be afraid to skip over this chapter if you're already comfortable with the material. You can always refer back to this material throughout your reading of this and other books, and when putting our lessons into practice.

LESSON 1
Avoid taxes, but don't evade them.

You might get away with murder, but you'd be hard pressed to get away with tax evasion – just ask Al Capone who was convicted of evasion (but not murder) on March 13, 1931 for side-stepping $251,748.93 in taxes. Evasion is a difficult thing to cover up once Revenue Canada's Special Investigations Unit is tipped off. *Tax evasion* is a deliberate attempt to reduce taxes owing by making false statements about your income or deductions, or by the destruction of records. Evasion is penalized by a fine of 50% of the tax evaded, plus interest from the year of the crime until payment is made, and can be accompanied by criminal charges filed by Revenue Canada which could result in additional penalties of 50% to 200% of the tax evaded and up to five years in prison. Prison is not just an empty threat; prison terms *have* been handed out to evading taxpayers in Canada. Needless to say, you'll probably want to avoid this situation.

Avoidance is something different altogether. *Tax avoidance* is simply exercising your right to minimize your taxes by way of proper tax planning. Proper tax planning could include taking advantage of *loopholes* which are inadvertent errors in the tax legislation, but more commonly involves taking advantage of existing provisions in the Income Tax Act to minimize taxes.

What We Have Learned:
* *tax evasion is illegal but tax avoidance is legally exercising your right to minimize your taxes.*
* *tax evasion brings stiff penalties and potential imprisonment.*
* *tax avoidance takes advantage of loopholes and existing provisions in the Income Tax Act to reduce your tax bill.*

LESSON 2
Monitor your marginal tax rate and your effective tax rate annually.

The Canadian tax system is *progressive* in nature (a term which we have always had a philosophic problem with since taxation isn't *progressive* in the usual sense). This means that the higher your income, the higher the percentage you'll pay in income taxes. For example, in 1996 an individual earning $25,000 per year in Ontario will pay tax at a marginal rate of 27.5%, while his neighbour earning $50,000 per year will pay tax at a marginal rate of 42.7%. The thinking behind this type of tax system is that wealthy individuals are supposedly able to bear a larger proportionate tax burden than those with more modest incomes. Canada is not the only country with a progressive tax system, in fact, most industrialized countries have adopted this type of system.

Your *marginal tax rate* is an important number and is simply the amount of tax you'll pay on your last dollar of income. Knowing your marginal tax rate will allow you to figure out your after-tax rate of return on your investments, or to calculate the tax savings from making an RRSP contribution or claiming deductions. Just to complicate things, your marginal tax rate will differ depending on the *type* of income earned. For example, interest, dividends, capital gains, and salaries or wages are each subject to different marginal tax rates. Appendix 2 at the back of this book details the marginal tax rates on each type of income at different income levels in each of the provinces.

Don't confuse your marginal tax rate with your average, or effective tax rate. Your *effective tax rate* is the rate of tax you pay on all of your taxable income. For example, if your taxable income (line 260 on your tax return) is $60,000 and your total taxes (line 435 on your return) are $20,000, then your effective tax rate is 33% ($20,000/$60,000). Note that your marginal tax rate in this case (at a taxable income of $60,000) would be 50.1% in Ontario. Knowing your effective rate becomes useful when you monitor it from year to year to see whether or not it's decreasing. Implementing even a few of the tax planning ideas in this book should result in a reduced effective tax rate over time. Your marginal rate, unlike your effective rate, is fixed by statute.

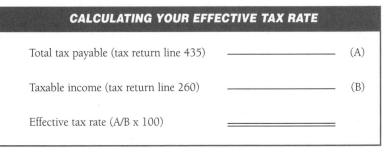

CALCULATING YOUR EFFECTIVE TAX RATE		
Total tax payable (tax return line 435)	——————————	(A)
Taxable income (tax return line 260)	——————————	(B)
Effective tax rate (A/B x 100)	══════════	

What We Have Learned:

- *your marginal tax rate is the amount of tax you'll pay on your last dollar of income.*
- *your effective tax rate is the amount of tax you pay on all your taxable income.*
- *you should monitor both rates each year and attempt to reduce your effective tax rate over time.*

LESSON 3

A tax deduction generally offers more relief than a tax credit.

A tax *deduction* reduces your net income in arriving at your taxable income. Your taxable income is then multiplied by the statutory tax rate to arrive at your taxes payable. A tax *credit* on the other hand is an amount that directly reduces your taxes payable.

	Net Income
Subtract	*Deductions*
	Taxable Income
Multiply	Tax Rate
	Taxes Payable
Subtract	*Credits*
	Net Taxes Payable

Which is better, a deduction or a credit? To make a long story short, if your taxable income is $29,590 or less, there's no difference between a deduction and a credit for you. If your taxable income exceeds $29,590, then deductions will offer more tax savings. The reason is that deductions will reduce your tax bill by your marginal tax rate times the deduction amount. For example, if your marginal tax rate is 52% and you claim a $1,000 deduction, your tax savings will be $520. On the other hand, a credit will reduce taxes by about 27%, so that a $1,000 credit will save you $270. If you earn $29,590 or less, your marginal tax rate will be about 27% so that the savings offered by a deduction and a credit will be about the same.

The point may not be all that useful except in the rare situation where you have a choice to claim either a deduction or a credit, but not both, for the same amount. This can happen, for example, when you have attendant care medical expenses that were necessary for you to earn business or employment income.

One last comment: charitable donation credits are generous and will, depending on your province, offer savings between 43% and 54% on contributions over $200 for the year, as compared to most credits at 27%. This makes contributions to registered charities as good as deductions for virtually all taxpayers, and actually better for those with lower incomes.

What We Have Learned:
- *a deduction usually offers more tax savings than a credit.*
- *a deduction and a credit are of equal value when your income is below $29,590.*
- *charitable donation credits are generous and are as good as any deduction if not better.*

LESSON 4

A dollar today is worth more than a dollar tomorrow.

Which would you rather have – a dollar today or a dollar tomorrow? Most people would instinctively take the dollar today – but do you know why this makes sense? Simply because you could take the dollar today, invest it, and end up with more tomorrow than just one dollar. This is called the time value of money, and we can apply the same line of thinking to your taxes. If you were offered $1.00 in tax savings today or the same savings one year from now, you would certainly take the savings today, because you could invest the savings and end up with $1.10 in one year – common sense. Likewise, if you had the choice between paying $1.00 in taxes today or paying that same $1.00 next year, you would of course pay it next year since you could invest the dollar for a year, end up with $1.10, pay the $1.00 in taxes next year and keep $0.10 for yourself. The time value of money is an important concept which will come up again and again as you plan to reduce your taxes.

What We Have Learned:
- *a dollar today is worth more than a dollar tomorrow.*
- *take tax savings today and make tax payments tomorrow.*

LESSON 5

Remember the five rules of thumb of tax planning.

The following is a list of five things you should always do if you hope to minimize your taxes. These are the five rules of thumb.

1. ALWAYS WAIT TO TRIGGER A TAX LIABILITY. Every time you dispose of capital property, switch your mutual funds, or undertake other similar transactions, you cause a taxable event to happen. There may be good reasons for entering these transactions, but keep in mind you may trigger a tax liability, and you don't want to owe taxes before you have to. Sometimes advisors who fail to focus on taxes will mistakenly omit this fact from the equation.

2. ALWAYS DELAY TAX PAYMENTS UNTIL REQUIRED. Once it has been established that you owe taxes, perhaps because you entered into a taxable transaction, *do not* pay your taxes until you are required to. For individuals, this date is April 30th of the year following the taxable event (unless you're required to make instalments – see lesson 105). If you're an employee and consistently receive refunds each April because of RRSP contributions, alimony payments, or other similar deductions, you should be applying to have the tax withheld from your pay reduced because you're making tax payments ahead of time. In effect, you're lending money to Revenue Canada, interest-free. Conversely, when you delay making your tax payments, it's a lot like receiving an interest-free loan from the government – and there aren't many places you can get a loan at zero interest.

3. ALWAYS THINK OF TAXES WHEN BIG LIFE-EVENTS OCCUR. It's very common to have clients walk through our doors with tax problems they didn't realize they had. Generally, people don't give much thought to taxes when they become involved in the following events. This list is not all-inclusive, but represents some of the situations that we believe require consultation with a tax professional:
a. a separation or divorce
b. establishment or revision of a will
c. start-up of a business
d. incorporation of a company
e. lending or giving money for business purposes

f. sale of a vacation property or investment real estate
g. purchase of vacation property or investment real estate
h. a move to the U.S. or elsewhere
i. spending more than four months a year in the U.S.
j. purchase of real estate located in the U.S. or elsewhere
k. carrying on business in the U.S. or elsewhere
l. a gift of capital property to a family member
m. inheritance of valuable property

4. ALWAYS PLAN FOR YOUR TAXES UPON DEATH. Realize that when you die, Revenue Canada wants one last dip into your pocket. All capital property that you own is deemed to be disposed of the moment before you die. This means that any property worth more at your death than what you paid will be subject to tax. Certain properties will transfer without any tax effect if left to a surviving spouse – for example, a jointly held home or cottage, an RRSP with your spouse as beneficiary, or any other property jointly held. If you expect to leave your family with a significant tax bill, you may want to buy life insurance to fund the tax liability. In any case, it's a good idea to know how much the taxman will want to take upon your death.

5. ALWAYS FIGHT THE TAXMAN. If you receive a Notice of Assessment from Revenue Canada that you disagree with, don't be afraid to fight them. You have one year from the due date of the disputed return to file a Notice of Objection, or 90 days after the date on the assessment, whichever is later. For example, if you disagree with your 1996 Notice of Assessment you have until April 30, 1998 to object (or 90 days after the date of the assessment if this is later). Your objection should be in writing and addressed to the Chief of Appeals at your district office. You can use Revenue Canada form T400A for this purpose if you want, but it's not required. In any case, your objection should state which year is at issue, the facts of the situation, the reasons for your objection, and how you'd like your assessment changed. Be sure to get a receipt from Revenue Canada as evidence that you filed the objection on time. Believe it or not, 77% of all objections filed on time result in a change being made in favour of the taxpayer, so it's worth the stamp to follow up.

What We Have Learned:
- *there are five rules of thumb to remember:*
  1. *Always wait to trigger a tax liability.*

2. *Always delay tax payments until required.*
3. *Always think of taxes when big life-events occur.*
4. *Always plan for your taxes upon death.*
5. *Always fight the taxman.*

LESSON 6
Understand what GAAR is, but never fear.

Avoiding taxes is perfectly legal, and evading taxes is blatantly illegal – a point we have already made. But there's a fine line between avoidance and evasion. There's no clear cut list of things you can and cannot do to avoid taxes. Some tactics are well within the law, and some, while within the letter of the law, are down-right aggressive.

To make life easier for itself, the government introduced the *general anti-avoidance rule* in 1988, affectionately known as GAAR. The rule says, in a nutshell, that where you're walking too closely to the thin line between avoidance and evasion Revenue Canada reserves the right, by law, to deny the use of your strategy.

It's Revenue Canada's policy that its local district offices cannot deny use of your strategy by invoking GAAR. Your local office must first transfer your case to the "GAAR committee" in Ottawa, and this will only be after you've had the chance to explain and defend your position at your district office. When defending your strategy at the district office level it will be important to put into writing your reasoning as to why your strategy should be allowed – this will make the job of the reviewer in Ottawa that much easier, which can only work to your benefit.

Don't let the thought of GAAR scare you. The worst that can happen if GAAR is invoked is that you'll be denied the tax strategy you implemented, and it has been a rare situation where GAAR has been applied.

What We Have Learned:
- *GAAR stands for the "general anti-avoidance rule" which permits Revenue Canada to deny, by law, any tax avoidance strategy you implement if it's too aggressive, even though you may be within the letter of the law.*
- *make all GAAR submissions to Revenue Canada in writing.*

- *do not fear, the worst that can happen is that your tax strategy will be disallowed, and it has been a rare situation where GAAR has been applied.*

LESSON 7

Know when and where to find professional tax advice.

There are certain occasions in life where we recommend that you seek the advice of an experienced tax professional. Refer to point 3 in lesson 5 for a list of thirteen such occasions. These cases complicate your life, and taxes can have various impacts in each situation. In particular, be aware of your probable need for help especially when you own your own business, sell a vacation property or investment real estate, establish or revise your will, spend a significant amount of time in the United States or elsewhere, when you leave Canada to live someplace else, or when you need to defend yourself against Revenue Canada (when GAAR is invoked, for example).

Who do you turn to for help? There are plenty of people out there who claim to be tax experts. Some of them are little more than tax preparers, and while they may do a fine job at preparing your tax forms, they may not have the expertise required to handle complex tax planning issues which is something different entirely. Still others may have accreditation in other fields, such as insurance, investments, or financial planning. These individuals usually have a basic understanding of income tax as it relates to their specific products, but generally do not have the expertise required to deal with complex tax issues and their interrelationship.

From our experience, complex tax issues should be handled by individuals who have completed the Canadian Institute of Chartered Accountants' In-Depth Tax Course. This is a two year course that is only offered to professionals who specialize in taxation. For the most part, these individuals will be chartered accountants or lawyers, although other professionals may attend. Not all chartered accountants and lawyers have taken the course, so when you approach a professional be sure to ask what their tax expertise is based on.

What We Have Learned:

- *there are certain occasions when you should seek the advice of a tax professional.*
- *complex tax issues should be handled by a tax professional who has completed the Canadian Institute of Chartered Accountants' In-Depth Tax Course.*

Part I

The Pillars *of* Tax Planning

Reducing Taxable Income

3

Reducing taxable income is the first of the four pillars of tax planning. When we talk about reducing taxable income, we're talking about doing one of three things: (1) claiming a deduction against income, (2) increasing your take-home pay or benefits without increasing the income you must report on your tax return, or (3) reporting taxable benefits in income but reducing your out-of-pocket costs at the same time. In this third case, we're not actually reducing your taxable income in most situations, but we're putting more money in your pockets by providing you with taxable benefits for things you might have purchased with your own money anyway – the effect is the same as if we had reduced your taxable income, so we've included these ideas here.

Deductions Against Income

As far as deductions go, are you claiming all that you're entitled to? Perhaps, but compare yourself to others in your income range. The following data shows total deductions as a percentage of income for different income classes and represents the most recent data available from Revenue Canada. To assess yourself, calculate your percentage by subtracting line 260 on your tax return from line 150 and dividing the result by line 150.

CALCULATING YOUR DEDUCTION PERCENTAGE

	Line 150 from tax return	———————	(A)
Less	Line 260 from tax return	———————	(B)
	Total Deductions (A – B)	———————	(C)
	Deduction percentage (C/A x 100)	———————	

AVERAGE DEDUCTIONS TAKEN BY CANADIANS

Income Level			Deduction Percentage
$ 6,750	to	$ 20,000	8.2%
20,001	to	30,000	8.6%
30,001	to	40,000	8.8%
40,001	to	50,000	9.7%
50,001	to	60,000	10.5%
60,001	to	70,000	11.5%
70,001	to	80,000	13.3%
80,001	to	90,000	13.7%
90,001	to	100,000	13.9%
100,001	and	over	17.3%

An interesting pattern emerges. The higher the income, the higher the deductions taken as a percentage of income. Obviously higher income earners are creating more deductions for themselves. You might argue that they're taking advantage of professional tax advice, and from our experience, you're probably right.

The good news is that we'll be introducing many of the tax planning ideas we recommend to our clients so that you too can take advantage of them. Many of the high income earners who are claiming larger deductions are also receiving compensation and benefits that are not even reported as taxable income on their returns because they have taken advantage of incentives provided in the Income Tax Act, and we'll be discussing some of these in this chapter as well.

LESSON 8

Claim all deductions allowed by employees under the law.

Unfortunately the Income Tax Act does not give employees much of a break when it comes to deductions. In fact, these deductions are limited to a few very specific situations. You'll need to obtain forms T2200 and T777 (not contained in the normal package) from your district taxation office and file them with your return to claim some of these deductions. The deductions to look for include:

1. SALESPERSON. Any costs necessary to earn commission income can be deducted up to the amount of those commissions. Some membership fees and depreciation on capital assets (except automobiles) are not deductible. See point 5 below for comments regarding your home-office.

2. AUTOMOBILE COSTS. Where you were ordinarily required to use your own vehicle for your employment, and did not receive a reimbursement or non-taxable allowance, you can claim a portion (based on business usage) of all automobile costs. Lesson 94 deals with automobile costs.

3. SUPPLIES. Where you were required to pay for your own supplies consumed directly in the performance of your duties these costs can be deducted. These costs include long-distance phone calls and cellular phone air time, but do not include phone connection or monthly service charges.

4. TRAVEL COSTS. Where you were required to pay your own travel costs (planes, trains, taxis, hotels, etc.) that were necessary under your employment contract or as stated by your employer on form T2200, and did not receive a reimbursement or a non-taxable allowance, you can deduct those costs.

5. WORK SPACE IN HOME. If an office in your home is where you principally perform your duties, or where the space is used to meet customers on a regular basis, you can deduct a portion of the following home costs: heat, hydro, and associated repairs and maintenance. Additionally, if you're an employed salesperson (point 1 above), you can also deduct a portion of your property taxes and insurance. As

discussed in lesson 93, those who are self-employed will be entitled to even more deductions, including a portion of mortgage interest and capital cost allowance.

6. OFFICE RENT. Where you were required by your employer to pay your own office rent you can deduct the rent costs. This does not include rent for space in your own home. See point 5 for work space in your home.

7. ASSISTANT'S SALARY. Where you were required to pay for an assistant, all salary or wages, CPP and UIC payments are deductible.

8. PROFESSIONAL OR UNION DUES. The cost of such dues are deductible where they were required to maintain a professional status recognized by provincial statute or membership in a trade union.

9. ARTIST'S COSTS. Where you have earned income from an artistic activity you can deduct costs associated with earning that income up to certain limits.

10. MUSICAL INSTRUMENTS. Where you were employed as a musician you can deduct (up to the amount of your income) the maintenance, rental, insurance, and capital cost allowance on your instruments.

11. LEGAL COSTS. When costs were incurred to collect or establish a right to salary, wages, alimony, or maintenance payments, these costs can be deducted. In addition, legal or accounting costs associated with filing a Notice of Objection or an appeal in a fight with Revenue Canada can also be deducted.

12. AIRCRAFT COSTS. Where you supplied your own aircraft for employment purposes and did not receive a reimbursement or non-taxable allowance, you can deduct a portion (based on business usage) of all aircraft costs.

13. ATTENDANT COSTS. Where you have a severe and prolonged impairment you can deduct up to 2/3 of earned income to a maximum of $5,000 for attendant care costs for yourself. The attendant cannot be your spouse or a minor. You won't be able to claim a medical expense credit for costs deducted as attendant costs.

14. CLERGY RESIDENCE. Where you're a member of the clergy you may be entitled to a deduction equal to the value of fair market rent on your residence. This deduction is available regardless of whether you rent or own your residence.

Note that where you have claimed a deduction for any of the above costs, you may be eligible to claim a rebate of the GST on those costs. File form GST 370 with your tax return and claim an amount on line 457 of your return. The rebate is taxable in the following year.

What We Have Learned:
- *deductions available to employees are limited to a few specific situations.*
- *file forms T2200 and T777 where applicable.*
- *you may be eligible for a GST rebate on deducted expenses by filing form GST 370.*

LESSON 9

↓ $

Take a deduction for RRSP contributions.

We won't go into much detail about RRSPs here since we'll be spending a whole chapter (chapter 7) on them later. We'd like to remind you that you're eligible to claim a deduction for any contributions to your RRSP up to certain limits (see lesson 53). Further, the timing of the deduction is completely up to you. That is, you don't have to take a deduction for your contributions in the year you make the contribution. You can take the deduction, for example, in a year when your marginal tax rate is higher, which will save you more tax dollars (lesson 61 talks more about this).

What We Have Learned:
- *you can claim a deduction for any RRSP contributions, up to certain limits.*
- *you don't have to take the deduction in the year you make the contribution.*
- *chapter 7 will deal more thoroughly with this topic.*

LESSON 10

Make your interest deductible and claim all carrying charges.

Interest Costs

Interest becomes deductible when the borrowed funds are used to earn investment income or income from a business. You should try to make as much interest as possible deductible for tax purposes. Many people, for example, own investment assets that are virtually debt-free while they own personal assets, like a home or cottage, with a mortgage or similar debt outstanding. In this case, taxable income is earned from the investment while non-deductible interest is paid on the loan.

A solution is to sell the investments and use the proceeds to pay down the existing debt; you can then borrow against the home or cottage and use the loan proceeds to purchase new investments. The interest on the newly borrowed funds becomes tax deductible since the funds were used to earn investment income. The deduction is claimed on line 221 of your return. Note that interest on loans to invest inside your RRSP is not deductible.

It used to be that if your investment went sour and you had borrowed money to acquire the investment, the interest on the continuing debt would no longer be deductible. The law changed beginning January 1, 1994 to permit the continued deduction of a portion of the interest on the continuing debt. Be sure to visit your tax professional to determine the portion still deductible since the rules are complex – the answer is usually well worth the cost of your visit.

Carrying Charges

Certain costs associated with earning investment income are deductible. These include:
- investment counsel fees
- investment management fees
- safe custody fees
- safe deposit box fees
- accounting fees for record keeping and investment advice
- broker asset management fees

- RRSP administration fees where they are personally paid outside your RRSP
- fees related to acquiring loans for investment purposes

These deductions are listed on schedule 4 and claimed on line 221 of your return.

What We Have Learned:

- *convert non-deductible interest to deductible interest where you have debt-free investment assets and debt-laden personal assets.*
- *you may be eligible to continue deducting some interest on money borrowed for an investment that went sour.*
- *claim a deduction for all carrying charges associated with earning investment income.*

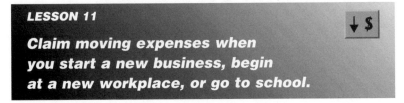

LESSON 11

Claim moving expenses when you start a new business, begin at a new workplace, or go to school.

When you start a new business, begin working from a new workplace, or attend a post-secondary institution full-time, you'll be entitled to deduct necessary moving expenses where your new home is at least 40 kilometres closer to your new place of work or school than your old home.

Deductible expenses include, but are not limited to, travel costs as well as related meals and lodging for up to 15 days, the cost of moving or storing household effects, lease cancellation costs at the old home, costs of selling the old home, legal fees related to purchasing the new home, and any land transfer taxes on the purchase of the new home. There are limits to the amounts you can deduct in the year of your move (one of these limits is the amount of your income earned at the new location), although undeducted amounts can be deducted in the subsequent year subject to certain limitations. Be sure to obtain form T1M from your local tax office and file it with your return for the year of your move, even if you're not deducting the full amount of your expenses in that year.

What We Have Learned:
- *where your new home is 40 kilometres closer to your new place of work or school than your old home you can claim a number of expenses against your income.*
- *there are limits to the amount you can deduct in a given year.*
- *be sure to file form T1M with your return in the year of your move.*

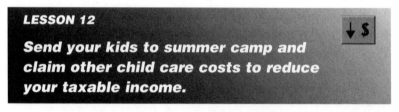

LESSON 12

Send your kids to summer camp and claim other child care costs to reduce your taxable income.

Certain child care costs can be deducted by you or your spouse so long as the costs were incurred to allow the earning of employment or self-employment income, training allowances, or research grants. Be careful, the deduction must generally be claimed by the lower income supporting person, and form T778 must be filed with the tax return. If one spouse's income is nil, then the other spouse can claim the deduction. The deduction will be limited to the least of three amounts:
- $5,000 per child who was not yet 7 years on December 31st, or for a child 7 years or over who has a severe and prolonged physical or mental infirmity,
- $3,000 per child for unimpaired children who were 7 years old but not yet 15 years on December 31st, or
- two-thirds of your earned income for the year.

Payments made to a summer camp or boarding school will qualify up to $150 per week per child who is severely impaired or under age 7, and up to $90 per week for children between 7 and 14 years who are unimpaired. Be sure to claim part-weeks in your camp calculation. Other deductible expenses include baby-sitting and day-care.

The higher income spouse can claim a deduction where the lower income spouse was at school full time, in a prison or similar institution for not less than two weeks in the year, certified to be incapable of caring for children, confined for at least two weeks to a bed or wheelchair, or living separate and apart at the end of the year for a period of at least 90 days as a result of marriage breakdown. The deduction available to the higher income spouse is limited to $150 per week for each child under 7 or impaired, and $90 for children between 7 and 14 years.

Be sure to include all of your children who were under age 15 on December 31st in your child care calculation since the taxman won't trace expenses to specific children. Doing this will expand the base for your claim. Consider John and Sue.

Taking care of John and Sue

John is 8 years old while his sister Sue is 12 years old. John's parents spent $5,000 in the year on his child care, and spent $100 ($50 for each child) in joint baby-sitting costs for John and Sue together. You might expect their parents to claim the maximum $3,000 in child care costs for John ($3,000 is the maximum since he's between age 7 and 15 and is not impaired) and another $50 for Sue's share of the baby-sitting costs, for a total of $3,050. In fact, the amount claimed should be much higher. You see, there are two children in the family who are between the ages of 7 and 15, and John and Sue's parents are allowed a maximum $3,000 deduction for each of them, for a total maximum deduction of $6,000. The taxman won't trace child care costs to specific children, so the full $5,100 spent on child care ($5,000 for John plus $100 in joint baby-sitting) can be claimed since it's less than the $6,000 maximum. In effect, we have allocated a portion of John's child care costs to Sue and increased the deduction by $2,050 ($5,100-$3,050). At a marginal tax rate of 50%, the taxes saved would be $1,025!

What We Have Learned:

- **child care costs can be deducted up to certain limits depending on the age of your child and whether or not he has an impairment.**
- **the types of costs deductible vary, and include summer camp fees among others.**
- **the taxman won't trace costs to specific children, so be sure to include all children under age 15 on your return to maximize your deduction.**

LESSON 13

Claim a deduction for your investment in a small business gone sour.

There are lots of people out there who have loaned money to family, friends, and strangers to help out in a business. It's a common occurrence for this money to be lost forever. So what can you do if you've invested in the shares of, or loaned money to, a small business corporation and the business has gone sour? In this event, any shares or debt in the company can be written-off as an *allowable business investment loss (ABIL)*. The amount that you can deduct is limited to 75% of the value of the shares or debt, but the amount can be deducted against any other source of income. The loss can be carried back three years or forward seven years if you can't use it in the current year to reduce your tax bill. After seven years, the loss will turn into a *net capital loss* if not used, and can then be applied against any future capital gains (but not other income). You could face some restrictions in claiming an ABIL where you've used any part of your capital gains exemption in the past, so visit a tax professional if you've got such losses.

What We Have Learned:
- *where you have invested in the shares of, or loaned money to, a small business corporation, and the business has gone sour, you can claim an allowable business investment loss (ABIL).*
- *there may be some restrictions where you have used all or part of your capital gains exemption.*

LESSON 14

Employee stock options can provide a 25% deduction against employment income.

Where your employer is willing to offer stock options as part of your compensation package, you could save yourself a bundle in taxes compared to straight salary. They work this way: your employer grants you a stock option which gives you the right to purchase, at some point in the future, shares of the company that employs you. The option will specify the price at which you can exercise the option (the *exercise price*). Assuming the fair market value of the shares when you acquire them is higher than the exercise price you pay, you can turn around and sell them back to your employer or to a third party at a profit. The gain is taxed as employment income in the year you *exercise* the option unless the company is a Canadian Controlled Private Corporation (CCPC) in which case you won't be taxed until you *dispose of* the shares acquired under the option. In either case, you may be entitled to claim a deduction (on line 249 of your return) equal to 25% of the gain when certain conditions are met.

Oliver's Option

Oliver Option was granted one stock option by his employer Money Inc. The option allowed Oliver to purchase one share in Money Inc. for $10 at any time during his employment with Money Inc. The fair market value of one Money Inc. share at the time the option was granted was $10. Two years later, with Oliver's hard work, one share of Money Inc. was worth $20, and Oliver decided to exercise his stock option. He purchased a share of Money Inc. for $10 (the exercise price) and then sold the share on the open market for its fair market value of $20. Alternatively, Oliver could have held onto his Money Inc. share for a while. In this case however, Oliver sold and made $10 on the deal. The $10 profit is considered to be employment income, however the Income Tax Act permits at deduction of 25% of the profit, or $2.50, against the income. Effectively, Oliver receives the $2.50 tax-free.

Stock options are a good idea if two conditions exist: (1) you're confident that the value of your employer's shares will increase (something you may have an influence on as an employee), and (2) you're able to sell the shares after exercising the option. These conditions are easier to meet if your employer is a large public company, although private companies have been known to issue stock options as well. The tax rules, as presented here, have been simplified, so be sure to visit a tax professional before you grant or exercise stock options to ensure you'll be entitled to the 25% deduction.

What We Have Learned

- *stock options can provide a 25% deduction against employment income resulting in lower taxes than straight salary.*
- *stock options are a good idea if you're confident the shares in your employer will increase in value, and where you're able to sell the shares at some point in the future.*

LESSON 15

↓ $

Stock appreciation rights, like stock options, can provide a 25% deduction against employment income.

Stock appreciation rights (sometimes called a *phantom stock plan*) are much like stock options (lesson 14) except that shares do not change hands, and consequently are more simple than stock options. They work this way: your employer grants you a stock appreciation right which you may exercise at some point in the future. The right will have an *exercise price*, and any increase in the value of your employer's shares above the exercise price will be paid to you in cash at the time of exercising the right. The income will be taxed as employment income, however you may be eligible for a deduction equal to 25% of the income, making just 75% of the income taxable.

Ralph's Right

Ralph Right was granted a stock appreciation right by his employer Profit Inc. The right had an exercise price of $50, and the value of one share in Profit Inc. was $50 at the time the right was granted. One year later, a share of Profit Inc. rose to $90 and Ralph decided to exercise his right. Upon exercising the right, Profit Inc. paid Ralph $40, the difference between the exercise price of $50 and the fair market value of $90. The $40 cash payment is taxable to Ralph as employment income, however he's entitled to a deduction of 25%, or $10, on his tax return. Ralph received the $10 tax-free.

Stock appreciation rights are a good idea if you're confident that your employer's shares will increase in value over time. Unlike stock options, there's no need to worry about whether you'll be able to sell the shares or how you'll finance their purchase, since you won't acquire any in this case.

What We Have Learned:
- *stock appreciation rights are more simple than stock options but can provide the same benefits – a 25% deduction against employment income.*
- *rights are a good idea where you expect the value of your employer's shares to increase over time.*

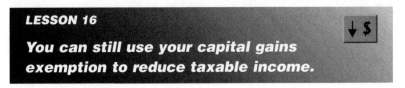

LESSON 16

You can still use your capital gains exemption to reduce taxable income.

Is the capital gains exemption really gone for good? Not quite yet. Even though filing your 1994 tax return represented the last opportunity to use your $100,000 lifetime exemption, you can still make a change to your 1994 tax return if you failed to use the exemption. There will be a penalty involved in electing to use the exemption at this late stage, but it may still be worth the cost if you have a large gain to shelter. Don't forget, you can only shelter gains that accrued up to February 22, 1994. A late election can be filed up until April 30, 1997. You can amend or revoke an election up until December 31, 1997.

It's important to note that where you own shares in a small business corporation or an operating farm you may be entitled to an enhanced capital gains exemption of $500,000 which, by the way, has not yet been done away with. This exemption can shelter any gain accrued on your shares if they qualify. The rules surrounding this exemption are complex, but your tax savings could be as high as $200,000, so a visit to your tax professional for details will be worthwhile.

What We Have Learned:
- *the $100,000 lifetime capital gains exemption will be available until April 30, 1997 to shelter gains accrued up to February 22, 1994.*

- *there will be a penalty for filing a late election to use the capital gains exemption.*
- *owning shares in a small business corporation or farm could entitle you to an enhanced capital gains exemption of $500,000 which has not yet been done away with.*

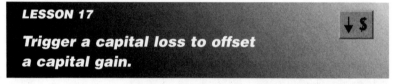

LESSON 17

Trigger a capital loss to offset a capital gain.

For those who hold investments outside an RRSP, there's the possibility that you may have realized a capital gain if you sold any of your investments at a profit. Unlike the good old days when your lifetime capital gains exemption would have sheltered your gain from tax, you'll pay tax on 75% of that gain now.

There's still a way to shelter that gain from tax – with capital losses. If you were to sell another investment that has an accrued loss, that loss could be used to offset the capital gain you've realized on your first investment. The best situation is where you sell the second investment at a loss in the same year you realized the gain on your first investment, enabling you to offset the gain with the loss on the same tax return. Keep in mind that where you're disposing of marketable securities to trigger a capital loss, you'll have to call your broker by about December 22nd to make the trade – this will ensure that settlement of the trade will happen before December 31st. If you failed to trigger a loss in the year of your capital gain, you can still do the following: recognize a loss by selling the second investment, then carry that loss back to one of the three preceding years to offset any capital gains in those years.

You'll have to watch out for the *superficial loss rules*, which will deny you use of the loss today where you sell an investment and then repurchase it at any time in the 30 days before or after the sale. You can get around these rules by purchasing a similar, but not the same, investment. Before triggering a loss to offset any realized gains, you should consider whether it might be better to hold the investment with the hope that its value might recover.

What We Have Learned:

- *where you have realized capital gains in a year, consider triggering a capital loss by selling another investment to shelter the gain from tax.*
- *watch out for the superficial loss rules.*
- *consider whether it might be better to hold your "loser" with the hope that its value might recover.*

LESSON 18

Add reinvested mutual fund distributions to your adjusted cost base to reduce gains.

With the popularity of mutual funds at a peak, it's important for you to understand how these investments are taxed if you're going to hold any of these funds outside your RRSP. If you own units in a mutual fund, you'll get a T3 slip each year (often not until April) detailing your share of any interest, dividends, capital gains, or other income that the fund realized in the year. You're required to pay tax on these *distributions*, even where you've reinvested them. You might also face a tax bill when you sell or switch your mutual funds. This will be the case where your mutual funds have increased in value since you bought them. If you're not careful, you could end up paying tax twice on the same income! Here's how.

Your mutual fund could increase in value each year as it earns interest, dividends, and capital gains. Some of this income, which is driving up the value of the fund, is taxed in your hands each year as you file the T3 slip with your tax return. Now, when you sell your units in the mutual fund, you'll have a capital gain to report on your tax return when you sell them at the increased value. The problem is, you've already paid tax on some of the income that gave rise to that increased value. This could mean double taxation for you.

To avoid this double tax problem, you'll have to keep track of all the *reinvested* distributions reported to you on your T3 slips each year and add these amounts to your cost (called your *adjusted cost base*) of the mutual funds. By doing this, your calculated capital gain will be lower when you actually sell the mutual fund units. For example, if you paid $100 for your mutual funds in 1996 and received reinvested distributions of $10 in 1996 and another $10 in 1997, then your new cost becomes $120. When you sell the mutual funds in 1998 for, say, $200, your gain is only $80 ($200-$120), not $100 ($200-$100). Your distributions can be tracked by keeping copies of your T3 slips each year, or by simply referring back to the statements you've received from the mutual fund.

What We Have Learned:
- *track your reinvested mutual fund distributions and add these to your adjusted cost base of your mutual funds to avoid double taxation.*
- *track distributions by keeping copies of T3 slips or referring to mutual fund statements.*

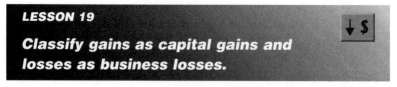

LESSON 19

Classify gains as capital gains and losses as business losses.

Tax law certainly is rife with grey areas, and the most common grey area taxpayers run across is simply this – whether to classify gains and losses as income or capital. In many cases it won't be clear whether you've got business income or a capital gain. Or, for that matter, a business loss or a capital loss.

Bill's Trading Habits
Bill works full-time for his employer, but is an avid fan of the stock and bond markets and tries to supplement his income by trading in securities. On average, Bill makes about seven trades each month. In 1996 Bill had a good year and made $25,000 on his trading – this was over and above his employment income. It's not clear whether the $25,000 gain represents a capital gain or business income. Bill could argue either way – and he'll want to take the position that will minimize his taxes.

Capital gains are only 75% taxable while business income is fully taxed. As a result, you'll want to argue that your gains are capital gains, not business income. Conversely, capital losses are of limited use since they can only be applied to shelter capital gains from tax, while business losses can be applied against any other type of income. So, if you've got losses, you'll want to try to classify them as business losses.

There are two important points to remember. First, you'll have to be consistent in your treatment of gains and losses. You can't, for example, call your stock market *gains* capital gains and your *losses* business losses – the taxman won't like this much. Another example is where you're buying and selling real estate on a regular basis and call your *gains* capital gains and your *losses* business losses. Consistency is important. Second, you'll want to ensure you have documentation to support your filing position. For example, if you sell a piece of real estate at a profit, you'd be wise to compile evidence that your intention was not to speculate and flip the property for a profit, but that you intended, for example, to rent the property out, or to live there yourself; this type of documentation will support your claim that your gain is a capital gain, and not business income. With the proper documentation, you'll be better able to discuss the issue with Revenue Canada, and file a Notice of Objection if necessary, should they decide to reassess your filing position. Visiting a tax professional will certainly help if Revenue Canada wants to argue with you.

One last point. You can elect to have all your gains and losses from buying and selling securities treated as capital in nature where you're not considered to be a trader (the term *trader* is not defined in the tax legislation). This can be done by filing form T123 with your tax return. The election needs to be made just once since it will remain in effect for all subsequent years (no changing your mind later). We'd recommend caution before making this election since it's not revocable, and you'll lose the opportunity of arguing that certain losses are business losses. Besides, you'll often be able to argue capital gains treatment for your gains, even without the election. Visit your tax professional before making this election.

What We Have Learned:
- *the most common grey area in tax is the classification of gains and losses as either income or capital.*
- *classify gains as capital gains and losses as business losses where possible.*

- *be consistent in your treatment of gains and losses from the same types of transactions, and compile documentation to support your filing position.*
- *you may be able to elect to treat all gains and losses from trading securities as capital in nature – but be careful because this election is not revocable.*

LESSON 20

↓ $

Claim business and professional losses as an effective way to reduce taxable income.

Running your own business, even a small one, can provide you with valuable tax write-offs. Does this mean giving up your day job? Absolutely not. Many people have skills or talents to offer others on a part-time basis. You may, for example, know enough about plumbing to offer your services to others. Perhaps you have the ability to make crafts that others would be willing to buy. The list is endless. As long as you're carrying on a bona fide business with a reasonable expectation of profit at some point in the foreseeable future, you'll be entitled to some attractive deductions against that income – note that Revenue Canada insists the business have a reasonable expectation of profit. See lesson 91 for more information on this expectation of profit requirement.

If your deductions exceed your income in your first few years of business, as is often the case, your losses can be applied against employment or other income. You will not be able to create or increase a business loss with home office expenses, but these costs can still be used to reduce your business income to zero, and unclaimed home expenses can be carried forward for future use.

A home based business may be one of the best ways to write-off a portion of your personal assets provided they are legitimately used in the business. The business will also permit you to split income with family members when they contribute time and effort to the business. We have devoted chapter 8 to self-employment where we'll talk more about the types of write-offs available in lessons 92 to 96. Here are some examples of home businesses you might consider:

- auto mechanics
- baby-sitting
- bookkeeping
- carpentry/renovations
- crafts
- desktop publishing
- electrical work
- fitness consulting

- freelance artist
- freelance editor
- lawn maintenance
- photography
- plumbing
- tax preparation
- tutoring
- word processing

What We Have Learned:
- *running a part-time home-based business can provide attractive write-offs.*
- *there's no need to give up your day job.*
- *there should be a reasonable expectation of profit in the foreseeable future to validate deductions.*

LESSON 21

Invest excess cash in a limited partnership.

↓ $

Some limited partnerships can provide attractive deductions in the first years of their existence. Keep in mind that you should exercise caution before putting your money into one of these tax shelters. You should only use money you don't mind playing with, and the underlying investment had better be a good one, or you risk losing $5,000, or whatever your investment is, for the sake of saving half that in taxes. Mutual fund limited partnerships are among the safest shelters. See lesson 118 for more details on limited partnerships.

What We Have Learned:
- *limited partnerships can offer attractive deductions in their first years of existence.*
- *the underlying investment ought to be a good one.*
- *mutual fund limited partnerships are among the safest.*

LESSON 22

File an adjustment when you've forgotten a deduction.

Now and again we'll have clients walk in with information that should have been included in a tax return filed three years ago. Sometimes the new information will even reduce the client's tax bill for that prior year. If you're in the situation where you now realize that you forgot to claim a deduction for something, you may be able to file an adjustment to your tax return for the year in question.

Generally, you'll be able to file an adjustment for any particular tax return within three years from the date on the original Notice of Assessment issued by Revenue Canada. Technically, the taxman is not obliged to honour your adjustment request unless you file the request within the required time limits for a Notice of Objection (the later of one year from the due date of the return or 90 days after the Notice of Assessment or Reassessment – see lesson 5 point 5). Filing within the three year time limit will not usually be a problem, although we'd recommend filing within the Notice of Objection time limits where you're claiming additional deductions. Adjustment requests can be made on a one-page form called T1ADJ which can be obtained from your local district taxation office.

What We Have Learned:
- *where you have forgotten to claim a deduction that you were entitled to claim, file an adjustment request as soon as possible, and certainly before three years has past since the original Notice of Assessment.*
- *use form T1ADJ to file an adjustment request.*

Non-Taxable Benefits

LESSON 23

Take part of your pay in the form of non-taxable benefits.

Many senior executives receive from 25% to 50% of their compensation in the form of non-taxable benefits, but many of these benefits are available, or could be available, to all employees. These benefits are very attractive because the value of the benefits will not show up on your T4 slip as taxable income – and there's nothing illegal about it! Often, these benefits are things you'd have to pay for out of after-tax income anyway, so receiving them tax-free is like receiving additional salary or wages.

Cindy Needs Day-care
Cindy's employer, Benefit Co., provides free day-care services to its employees. The value of the day-care over a one year period for one child is about $6,000. For Cindy to pay someone else to look after her son for a year, she'd have to earn an extra $12,000 to cover the cost assuming her marginal tax rate is 50% ($12,000 x 50% = $6,000). Since she pays nothing for the day-care, the tax-free benefit is equivalent to receiving an additional $12,000 in salary.

Here's a list of tax-free benefits that you might want to approach your employer with, particularly when you're negotiating or renegotiating salary or wages. To entice your employer to go along with the idea, consider taking a cut in pay equal to your employer's cost of these benefits. In this case, there's no additional cost to your employer, but you'll be better off because you won't be taxed on the benefit as you would with salary or wages. While some of these ideas are common, many are not.

1. MORTGAGE SUBSIDY PLAN. Such a plan will allow an employer to arrange mortgage financing for employees and make payments directly to the financial institution for a portion of the employee's interest cost. No taxable benefit will arise as long as the employee's interest cost after the subsidy remains at or above Revenue Canada's prescribed rate.

2. PERSONAL COUNSELLING. Costs paid by your employer for counselling related to the physical or mental health of you or a family member will be tax-free. In addition, financial or legal counselling related to your re-employment or retirement is also tax-free. So, if your employer paid for someone to explain the tax rules as they relate to your situation, the benefit to you would be tax-free.

3. EMPLOYER-PROVIDED DAY-CARE. The value of day-care provided by your employer will be received by you tax-free as we have mentioned.

4. SUBSIDIZED MEALS. Where your employer provides subsidized meals, there will be no taxable benefit as long as you are required to pay a reasonable charge. This charge will often be your employer's cost of the meal.

5. DISCOUNTS ON MERCHANDISE. Where you're able to purchase items from your employer at a discount there will not be a taxable benefit provided the discount is generally available to all employees.

6. COMMISSIONS ON SALES. If you've been paid a commission on the sale of a product purchased by you for your personal use, the commission is not taxable.

7. TRANSPORTATION TO YOUR JOB. Where your employer provides transportation to or from work for security or other reasons, the value of the transportation is a tax-free benefit. Note that an allowance or reimbursement for transportation you provide yourself is taxable.

8. USE OF RECREATIONAL FACILITIES. If your employer provides recreational facilities for your use, the benefit is tax-free.

9. MEMBERSHIP FEES. Membership fees for social and recreational clubs paid by your employer are tax-free as long as your employer expects to benefit from your membership.

10. UNIFORMS AND SPECIAL CLOTHING. If your employer provides you with a distinctive uniform or special clothing, including footwear, to be worn at work, the cost of such clothing, including laundry costs, is not taxable. So if you enjoy wearing that fluorescent orange lab coat out on the town, this benefit is multiplied.

11. RELOCATION EXPENSES. Your employer is able to reimburse you for the cost of moving as a result of a transfer or where your employer otherwise requires you to move closer to work without having the benefit taxed in your hands.

12. REIMBURSEMENT FOR LOSS ON SALE OF HOME. If your employer requires you to move and you incur a loss on the sale of your home, your employer can reimburse you for the amount of the loss without the benefit being taxable.

13. FAIR MARKET VALUE GUARANTEE. Your employer may require you to move and will guarantee that you'll receive fair market value for your home upon its sale. If, in this case, you must sell for less than the fair value and your employer makes up the difference, you will not be taxed on this benefit.

14. INTEREST SUBSIDY. This is similar to the mortgage subsidy mentioned in point 1, but differs in that it arises when your employer requires you to relocate. Where you're required to move to another city, your employer may be able to pay the additional interest costs where you're forced to take on a larger mortgage because the cost of housing is higher in your new location. Visit a tax professional if this applies to you.

15. DENTAL PLAN. Chances are you're already part of a group dental plan at work. The costs paid for by the plan, and the premiums paid for by your employer, are all tax-free benefits.

16. CONTRIBUTIONS TO CERTAIN GROUP PLANS. Where your employer makes contributions on your behalf to a group sickness or accident insurance plan, the contributions are not a taxable benefit. Any benefits received by you under these plans will be taxable. There's an exception: you can avoid being taxed on any payouts from these plans if *you* pay the premiums rather than your employer – something to consider.

17. CONTRIBUTIONS TO A PRIVATE HEALTH PLAN. Any contributions made by your employer to a private health plan are tax-free benefits to you.

18. GIFTS. Your employer might provide you with a gift at Christmas or on some other special occasion. You're allowed to receive up to $100 a year in gifts tax-free. If you're getting married, the total gifts in that year can add up to $200 tax-free.

19. EDUCATION COSTS. Where your employer pays the cost of courses taken by you, there will not be a taxable benefit where it can be presumed your employer is benefiting from your education. If your employer gives you paid time-off to attend classes and for study purposes it's presumed your employer is benefiting.

20. BUSINESS TRIP TURNED PERSONAL. Try turning a business trip into a personal vacation. If, for example, you're in Los Angeles for five days on business, your flight is paid for, so why not spend another week there vacationing? The cost of the flight will not be taxable to you since you have to come home from the business trip some time. Or, if a flight to Los Angeles is going to cost your employer $750 while a flight to Hawaii is $850, why not arrange to pay the additional $100 yourself and make a trip to Honolulu following business in Los Angeles? Pretty cheap vacation when you remove the air fare.

21. LEASED CLOTHING. Believe it or not, this became popular in the UK. If it's important to your employer that you're well dressed at all times, your employer can arrange with a clothier to lease clothing for your use. The clothing will be tailored to fit you specifically and will be given to you for a period of time, say three years. You'll have to keep the clothes clean and in good condition and return them at the end of the lease in three years, or upon termination of your employment. At the end of the lease term, you can purchase the suit from the clothier at its fair market value, which will be very low after three years of use – say $25. While the tax treatment will remain unclear until Revenue Canada makes a pronouncement, there's no doubt that the taxable benefit, if there is one at all, will still cost you far less than buying the clothing with after-tax dollars yourself.

22. ANY ITEM OF PERSONAL VALUE. Similar to the leased clothing example above, your employer can arrange to lease any number of things that you might also like to own – a computer, or an antique desk, for example. At the end of the lease term, you can arrange to buy the item from the dealer at its then current fair market value, which should be substantially lower than the original price. Your employer doesn't have to lease the item; it could be purchased outright with the understanding that you'll buy it from your employer later at its fair market value. Where the item is something your employer needed to lease or buy anyway, it may be very easy to make an arrangement to buy the item at a later date.

What We Have Learned:
- *receiving tax-free benefits in lieu of salary or wages can significantly reduce taxable income.*
- *such benefits are particularly attractive where they are things you would have purchased for yourself anyway.*
- *there are a number of creative benefits available to employees which should be considered when negotiating or renegotiating salary or wages.*

LESSON 24

Negotiate the payment of a tax-free death benefit.

↓$

As part of your compensation package consider negotiating with your employer to provide a tax-free death benefit to your spouse, children, or another beneficiary. The tax legislation will allow payments of up to $10,000 to be paid tax-free by your employer to your spouse or another beneficiary upon your death (your employer is permitted a deduction for the payment). Look at it as an insurance policy with no premiums. You won't be around to enjoy it, but your family will thank you.

What We Have Learned:
- *a $10,000 death benefit can be paid tax-free to your spouse or another beneficiary by your employer upon your death.*
- *this is much like receiving $10,000 of insurance without paying premiums.*

Taxable Benefits

LESSON 25

Even a taxable benefit is better than paying the cost yourself.

↓$

The idea here is that there are certain benefits your employer might provide you with that are taxable to you as income. Provided the benefit is something you would have purchased yourself anyway, you'll still be better off taking the benefit and paying tax on it than paying for the item or service yourself with after-tax dollars. The amount that you'll be taxed on is your employer's cost of the benefit being provided to you. So, where your employer is able to negotiate a favourable cost from a supplier, the savings are really passed on to you.

Graham's Vacation

A client of ours, Graham, received one free week at a condominium in Florida owned by his employer Condo Inc. The value of this benefit was

$500 which was included on his T4 slip as income (the amount included on his T4 will be his employer's cost). The cost to Graham was $250, the tax on his benefit, since his marginal tax rate is 50%. If Graham had rented the condo himself, it would have cost him $500 out of his own pocket. He's better off by $250 because it was provided as a taxable benefit.

Your savings from receiving something as a taxable benefit rather than paying for it yourself is simply the value of the benefit multiplied by one minus your marginal tax rate, as follows:

CALCULATING SAVINGS FROM A TAXABLE BENEFIT	
Value of taxable benefit	_____
Multiply by one minus your marginal tax rate	x (1-mtr)
Savings from the taxable benefit	_____

What We Have Learned:
- *receiving something as a taxable benefit from your employer is still cheaper than paying for it yourself.*
- *the savings is equal to the value of the benefit multiplied by one minus your marginal tax rate, if you care to calculate it.*

LESSON 26

Borrow money from your employer, not a bank.

By borrowing from your employer you may be able to save interest costs since the loan can be made at no or low interest. You'll be required to include an interest benefit in income, however you'll still be better off than borrowing from the bank. The taxable benefit will equal Revenue Canada's prescribed interest rate less the actual interest you pay on the loan. This benefit also applies if the loan is to a member of your family. Your payment of interest, if any, must be made on or before January 30th following the year the loan was out-standing.

Jennifer and her Computer

Jennifer received a $3,000 loan from her employer to purchase a home computer. The loan was at a low rate of just 3% although Revenue Canada's prescribed rate was 8%. Jennifer's T4 slip included a taxable benefit of $150 calculated as 5% (8% minus 3%) of $3,000. Tax on the $150 benefit was $75, assuming her marginal tax rate was 50%. Jennifer's total cost of borrowing was $165 ($75 tax on the benefit plus $90 in inter-est paid to her employer at 3%). If she had borrowed from the bank at 8%, her cost of borrowing would have been $240 ($3,000 x 8%). She saved $75 in interest by borrowing from her employer.

Commercial rate loans

If the interest rate charged by your employer is equal to or greater than the rate you could receive from an unrelated third party – a bank for example – there will be no interest benefit.

Home financing loans

There's good news if you borrow from your employer to purchase or refinance a home. In this case, the prescribed rate used to calculate your interest benefit will be the lesser of the current rate and the rate in effect at the time the loan was made. Every five years you're deemed to have received a new loan in this case, and so the prescribed rate in effect at that time will apply for the next five year period.

Home loan upon relocation

There's even better news if you borrow from your employer to pur-chase a new home upon a relocation to a new work place. In this sit-uation, you'll be entitled to a deduction for the interest benefit on the first $25,000 of the loan. This means that, when borrowing from your employer to purchase a home upon relocation, you can receive up to $25,000 without incurring a taxable interest benefit. This deduction is available where you were eligible to claim moving expenses, and for the first five years of the loan only.

Interest deduction available

An interest deduction equal to the amount of your interest benefit is available where you would have been entitled to deduct interest costs had you borrowed the money from a bank or another third party. This means that your employee loan might be tax-free where you borrowed to earn investment income or to purchase an automobile or aircraft.

Shareholder loans

Where you received a loan by virtue of your share ownership rather than as an employee you'll be subject to very restrictive rules that will include the amount of the loan in your income unless repayment has been made within one year after the end of the company's tax year. For this reason, where you're a shareholder of a company, it's very important that any loans to you arise as a result of your employment (and not your share ownership) and that bona fide arrangements for repayment within a reasonable time be made.

In addition, where you own 10% or more of the company, the loan should be for certain purposes only, namely: to acquire a home for yourself, to acquire treasury shares from the company, or to acquire a vehicle for use in your employment. If you're a shareholder borrowing from your company, be sure to visit your tax professional to structure the loan properly, or you could be in for an unpleasant tax hit.

What We Have Learned:

- *borrowing from your employer rather than the bank will save you money.*
- *there are special rules that could work to your benefit where you borrowed money to finance a home, to relocate, or to invest in income producing assets.*
- *shareholders who borrow money must structure the loans properly to avoid an unpleasant tax hit; visiting a tax professional is highly recommended.*

Splitting Taxable Income

4

$ | $

There seems to be a definite pattern emerging: if you make money, the taxman will be knocking at your door to collect some of it. The question is, who in your family should be paying tax on the earnings? The answer is easy – the person with the lowest marginal tax rate. In fact, your tax savings could be as high as 54%, depending on your province.

Jeremy and his daughter

Jeremy has $10,000 to invest. His investment advisor assures him that a 10% return is no problem this year. Jeremy will earn $1,000 at 10% and will pay taxes of $540 at a marginal tax rate of 54%. This leaves $460 in his pocket after taxes. Jeremy has heard that he may be able to arrange his affairs so that his 19 year old daughter will pay tax on the $1,000 income instead. His daughter's income will be under $6,500 this year, and so she'll pay no taxes at all – her marginal tax rate is zero. The tax savings to Jeremy is $540!

This brings us to the second pillar of tax planning, splitting taxable income. The idea is to move income that would otherwise be taxed at a higher rate to a person with a lower marginal tax rate. Revenue Canada has gone to great lengths to make sure that you're not abusive in splitting income. In this regard, they introduced the *attribution rules*, which will cause income to be taxed in your hands if you improperly try to pass it along to family members, including in-laws and nieces or nephews.

Specifically, the attribution rules will prevent you from lending or transferring property to your spouse to have interest, dividends, or capital gains taxed in his or her hands – the taxman will deem the income to have been earned in *your* hands, and you'll pay the tax. In addition, the rules are designed to prevent you from moving interest and dividends to your minor children, and in some cases, your adult children. Are there legal ways of getting around the attribution rules? Absolutely! What follows is a comprehensive list of income-splitting techniques that we're sure you'll find practical.

LESSON 27

Make a loan to your spouse or child to split income.

When you lend money or property to a spouse or child you retain ownership. The loan can bear interest, or be interest-free. Where no interest is charged, you may have to perform another step or two to dance around the attribution rules. The next seven ideas involve loans to family members.

1. MAKE A LOAN AT FAIR VALUE. The idea here is simple. Lend money to your spouse or child to invest and charge him or her interest at Revenue Canada's prescribed rate. Charging interest at regular commercial rates where those rates are less than the prescribed rate is ok with the government and makes good sense. When you charge interest, there's no attribution of income back to you. The interest must be paid to you by January 30th of the year following the loan, and must be included in your income. Your spouse or child can take a deduction for the interest paid to you. Where the income earned on the loaned funds is higher than the rate of interest paid to you, the excess is taxed in the hands of your spouse or child and you have effectively split income.

2. MAKE A BUSINESS LOAN. Where you lend funds to a family member to invest in a business, there will be no attribution of business income or gains back to you. There's no need to charge interest on a loan of this type. The business can operate as a proprietorship, partnership (except a limited partnership), or a corporation where it's a small business corporation.

3. MAKE A LOAN FOR OTHER THAN INVESTMENTS. The attribution rules will not apply where you lend money to your spouse or child for other than investment purposes. If, for example, you lend money to your spouse to pay her income taxes, this will free-up any income she might earn to invest for herself. The investment income will, of course, be taxed in your spouse's hands and you have effectively split income.

4. MAKE A LOAN THEN TAKE IT BACK. If you lend money to your spouse or minor child for investment purposes, the income will be taxed in your hands. But what about the second generation income – that is, income on the income? Second generation income will not be attributed back to you. Try this idea: lend funds, say $10,000, to your spouse or child for one year. The income in the first year, say $1,000, will be taxed in your hands. Now take back the $10,000 and leave the $1,000 in the hands of your spouse or child. Any income on the $1,000 will be taxed in their hands at, perhaps, a marginal tax rate of nil. To make this worth your while you may want to lend a larger amount than the $10,000 in our example, or alternatively, take the loan back only after four or five years have passed – this will leave more income in the hands of your spouse or child and increase the value of the idea.

5. LEND FUNDS TO A CHILD AND CHARGE ROOM AND BOARD. When you lend money to an adult child, there's generally no attribution. Since you may not want to give up your hard earned money to your 19 year old who might spend it on the finer things in life, you can charge him or her rent to recover the income earned on the loaned funds. Rent paid from a child to his parents is not taxable in the tax-man's view since you're related, and the arrangement is not considered to be profit-motivated. In addition, your child will be able to claim a credit for the rent paid to you where such credits are available in your province.

Bruce and His Son
Bruce loaned $5,000 to his 19 year old son who invested the money and earned a 10% return on the investment, or $500 for the year. Bruce's son will report the income (not Bruce) since the attribution rules do not gen-

erally apply to those children 18 years of age and over. Bruce's son does not earn more than $6,500 per year, so he will not pay taxes on the $500. Bruce then charged his son room and board of $480 for the year ($40 per month) which Bruce receives tax-free. Bruce did not charge his son rent exactly equal to the investment income his son earned since Revenue Canada may look through the transaction and would have a better argument, under GAAR (see lesson 6), that the income should be attributed back to Bruce.

6. MAKE A FAIR VALUE LOAN, THEN FORGIVE IT. The attribution rules will not apply when you charge fair value interest at Revenue Canada's prescribed rate on funds loaned to your spouse or child. So lend funds to a family member and collect interest for one year. After one year, forgive the loan. The amount of the loan forgiven will be included in the income of your spouse or child under the *debt forgiveness rules*, but where your spouse has little or no income, a loan of $6,500 can be forgiven without any tax to him or her. To make this work, the funds loaned to your spouse or child should be invested in nothing but a bank account for the first year while you are charging interest on the loan. The reason for this is that the debt forgiveness rules will only work in your favour if there was no capital property purchased with the loaned funds.

7. GIFT INTEREST EXPENSE. Many of the loan ideas we have mentioned will involve charging fair value interest on funds loaned to your spouse or child. If the family member borrowing the money is not able to make interest payments to you because he has little or no cash, consider giving him the cash necessary to make interest payments to you. The cash gift will not result in any attribution to you because the cash was not given to earn income. Revenue Canada may not appreciate this tactic, and so you might be in for an argument even though the provisions of the Income Tax Act would not prevent the manoeuvre.

What We Have Learned:
- *when you lend property to your spouse or child you retain ownership; loans can be interest-bearing or not.*
- *make a loan at fair value.*
- *make a business loan.*
- *make a loan for other than investments.*

- *make a loan then take it back later.*
- *lend funds to a child and charge room and board.*
- *make a fair value loan, then forgive it.*
- *gift interest expense.*

LESSON 28
Transfer cash or property to your spouse or child to split income.

There are effectively two ways of transferring property to a family member: (1) as a gift, or (2) by selling the property. This is, of course, different than a loan since the cash or property legally changes hands, although you don't have to give up control of the property where you set up a trust. The next six ideas involve the transfer of cash or property to split income.

8. SWAP ASSETS WITH A FAMILY MEMBER. This technique allows your spouse or other family member to pay tax on an investment that he or she "buys" from you with an asset of equal or greater value. Preferably, the assets you take back should be non-income-earning assets such as jewellery, a collection, or artwork. Thinking ahead can pay off here. Try putting some assets in the name of your spouse or child now so that a swap can be done easily at a later date. For example, a family home purchased in joint names is a large store of value for a swap later (although most provincial Family Law Act's would override any such sale to allocate one half of the home back to the selling party in the event of a marriage break-up). When doing a swap, you might trigger a capital gain if the property you transfer has appreciated in value, however capital gains are only 75% taxable and the future savings may very well justify the swap. Finally, many investments like Canada Savings Bonds and Guaranteed Investment Certificates should have no appreciation, and hence no tax when swapped.

9. GIFT CAPITAL GAINS TO YOUR CHILDREN. Regardless of your child's age, capital gains earned on investments are not attributed back to you. There are a few ways of putting investments in the hands of your child or grandchild. The easiest way is to give or lend your child cash to buy the investment. You might also transfer some of your investments to your child's name although you'd have a disposition for tax purposes which could give rise to some tax if the investment is worth more today than when you bought it. It might still be worth transferring the investment despite the tax since only 75% of the gain will be taxed, and the future tax savings may justify the idea.

10. TRANSFER ANY INVESTMENT TO YOUR ADULT CHILD. Investment income will not be attributed back to you where you transfer (by gift or sale) investments to a child or grandchild who has reached the age of 18 by the end of the year you make the transfer. This exception applies whether the investments are earning interest, dividends, capital gains, or a combination. One drawback is that you lose control of the investment since it becomes the property of your child. You might transfer the property to a trust with your adult child as the beneficiary so that you maintain control of the investment and still avoid the attribution rules to split income.

11. BUY A VACATION PROPERTY IN YOUR CHILD'S NAME. There may be times where it makes sense to buy a vacation property, like a cottage, in the name of your adult child. You see, when you own two properties, there's the possibility that tax could arise upon the sale of one of those properties where the property was sold at a profit. The reason for this is that each family is only entitled to one *principal residence exemption* – the exemption that allows you to sell your principal residence at a profit, tax-free. Your adult child is considered to be his or her own "family", and consequently entitled to a separate principal residence exemption once he or she is married or is 18 years of age.

Buying the cottage in your adult child's name will multiply the principal residence exemptions available to the household. Where the property is already owned by you, it may make sense to transfer the property to your adult child where the property hasn't appreciated much in value since buying it, and where you expect it to appreciate in value significantly over the next few years. You might also consider transferring the property to a trust to retain control while still providing another principal residence exemption. There are a number of issues to consider before trying these ideas, so be sure to visit a tax professional before you put any vacation property in the name of a child.

12. TRANSFER PROPERTY BEFORE LEAVING CANADA. This idea works well where you and your spouse have decided to leave Canada – perhaps to retire in the sunny south. Immediately prior to leaving Canada to become a resident elsewhere you are deemed to have disposed of certain capital property that you own. If that property has accrued gains attached to it, you might pay tax on those gains when you leave. Try this idea that we recommended to one of our clients – here's their story (names changed to protect the innocent).

Lucy and Ricky's Story
Lucy and Ricky decided that warmer climes were desirable and headed south last January. Ricky owned some stocks worth $5,000 more than his cost at the time they decided to move. On December 25th last year, just before leaving Canada, Ricky gave Lucy his stock portfolio (with no tax consequences to himself since she is his spouse and the stocks transferred to her at his original cost). On January 5th Ricky left for the south and became a resident of the U.S. Two days later Lucy left to be with him and gave up Canadian residency on January 7th. When Lucy left, she was holding the stocks with a $5,000 gain which was taxable upon her leaving. Normally, the gain would be taxed in Ricky's hands under the attribution rules, however, he was not resident in Canada when Lucy left the country and triggered the gain, and so the attribution rules did not apply to him. Lucy paid the tax on the gain at her lower rate, and the couple successfully split income. It's important to have a reason for one spouse to stay behind for a couple of days – to finalize a home sale or wrap up some paperwork at the office, for example.

13. LEAVE PROPERTY UPON YOUR DEATH. If you die with income producing property in your hands that transfers to your spouse or children there's no attribution to you or your estate. This is probably no surprise since it makes sense the taxman can't continue to tax you when you're gone. As you might guess, this income splitting technique is not a client favourite to implement.

What We Have Learned:
- *transfers entail gifting or selling property to a family member.*
- *a transfer means giving up ownership in your name, but not necessarily control of the property.*
- *swap assets with a family member.*
- *gift capital gains to your children.*

- *transfer any investment to your adult child.*
- *buy a vacation property in your child's name.*
- *transfer property before leaving Canada.*
- *leave property upon your death.*

LESSON 29

Give a deduction or credit to your spouse or child to split income.

Although giving a deduction or credit to a spouse or child is not quite the same as moving income from one tax return to the next, the effect on total taxes paid by the family is the same, and so we've included such ideas here.

14. TRANSFER PERSONAL TAX CREDITS TO THE HIGHER-INCOME SPOUSE. Certain personal credits can be transferred from the lower-income spouse to the higher-income spouse, which is effectively the same as moving income into the hands of the lower-income earner. In particular, where your spouse's taxable income is low enough, you may be able to transfer some or all of the following credits to your return: age credit (if your spouse was 65 years of age or older in the year), disability credit (where your spouse had a severe mental or physical impairment supported by your doctor's completion of form T2201), tuition and education credit, and the pension credit (where your spouse had some pension income).

15. TRANSFER MEDICAL EXPENSES TO THE LOWER-INCOME SPOUSE. The family's medical expenses can be claimed by either spouse. Since there's an income threshold over which you will not be eligible to claim any credit for your medical expenses, it will often be a good idea for the lower-income spouse to claim the expenses since he or she will get more tax relief where taxes are owing. As a family, you'll save tax dollars by doing this, which is tantamount to splitting income.

16. CLAIM ALL CHARITABLE DONATIONS ON ONE RETURN. Since the first $200 of donations claimed on each return only offers tax relief at 27% of the donation amount while the remaining donations offer relief at between 43% and 54%, it makes sense to maximize the donations at the higher rate. This can be done by claiming all donations on one tax return. Generally, we recommend the donations be claimed by the higher-income spouse, although your family will still be better off with the lower-income spouse claiming the donations than you'll be by claiming the donations on different returns.

17. TRANSFER CAPITAL LOSSES TO YOUR SPOUSE. Suppose you have an investment worth less today than what you paid – that is, you have an accrued capital loss. If you sell the investment to your spouse for its fair value, the taxman will deny you the loss on the sale. The *superficial loss rules* ensure that you can't create a loss, to use against capital gains, when you don't truly sell the investment – that is, when you merely sell it to your spouse or child. We can make this rule work in our favour. When you sell the investment to your spouse for its fair value, her cost of the investment becomes your original cost. Now your spouse is free to sell the investment on the open market. This creates a capital loss in her hands that can be used to offset any capital gains now or in the future.

Darren and Samantha
Darren owns 100 shares of ABC Company that he paid $5,000 for. Unfortunately, the shares are only worth $500 today giving him an accrued loss of $4,500. Darren's wife Samantha owns some shares of her own in XYZ Company that have magically done very well. She paid $1,000 for her stocks that are worth $5,500 today. Darren sold his shares to Samantha for their fair value of $500 and he is denied the $4,500 loss. Samantha acquired the shares for $500, but her cost for tax purposes is Darren's original cost of $5,000. Samantha then sold the shares for their value of $500 and realized a capital loss of $4,500. This capital loss can be used at any time in the future to offset capital gains. If she were to sell her XYZ shares for a profit, the gain would be sheltered with the capital loss, and she would not pay tax on the gain, which would preserve her capital to be reinvested.

You'll have to be sure not to involve a corporation, trust, or partnership in moving losses to your spouse or a related person since there are rules designed to prevent this. See your tax professional for more information.

What We Have Learned:
- giving a deduction or credit to a spouse has the same effect, in that taxes are reduced, as moving income to the lower-income spouse's return.
- transfer personal tax credits to the higher-income spouse.
- transfer medical expenses to the lower-income spouse.
- claim all charitable donations on one return.
- transfer capital losses to your spouse.

LESSON 30
Invest cash receipts in the right hands to split income.

$|$

Families can receive cash from any number of sources. It's important to ensure that the cash being invested is in the right hands, otherwise you'll pay more tax than you have a right to pay. The next four ideas should help to ensure some of your cash receipts are invested to minimize taxes.

18. INVEST CHILD TAX BENEFITS IN YOUR CHILD'S NAME. The family allowance system was replaced in January 1993 with the child tax benefit, but from the recipient's point of view, not much has changed – you're still entitled to monthly benefits for each child under 18. These benefits can be invested in the name of your child, and all income earned on the investments is taxable to your child – the attribution rules won't apply. Your child will not likely have enough income to be taxable, and so the benefits will compound tax-free. Makes for a good start to an education fund. Be sure to keep separate investments for each child and keep good records so that investment income can be traced back to the child tax benefit payments you received. If you have already spent these funds, then your child has, in effect, loaned to you the child tax benefits. This loan can be repaid, with interest, when you're in a position to do so, allowing your child to invest at his or her lower tax rate.

19. HIGHER-INCOME SPOUSE SHOULD PAY HOUSEHOLD EXPENSES. The idea here is that when the higher-income spouse pays all household expenses, any income of the other spouse is freed-up to invest. The result is that investment income is taxed in the hands of the lower-income spouse. You could even pay any income taxes owing by the lower-income spouse without fear of any attribution. While directly giving money to your spouse for investment purposes will be caught under the attribution rules, this idea accomplishes the same thing and gets around those rules.

20. INVEST INHERITANCES IN THE RIGHT NAME. If your lower-income spouse receives any type of inheritance be sure that the funds are kept in his or her name so that the resulting income is taxed at a lower rate. If an inheritance is received jointly by you and your spouse, be sure to invest the two halves separately, again, to ensure your spouse's half is taxed at his or her lower rate. By the way, most provincial Family Law Acts say that if your marriage breaks up later, inheritances that were invested separately in the name of the recipient will remain the property of the recipient spouse while funds invested in both names will be split.

21. GIVE A WORKING CHILD AN ALLOWANCE. Sounds like we're doing things in the wrong order – when your child is old enough to earn some money the allowances usually stop. Maybe they shouldn't. Try paying your child an allowance which will free-up his or her employment income for investment. Any investment income will now be taxed in your child's hands, with no attribution. You have effectively given your child income to invest and be taxed at a lower rate – and your child will probably pay no taxes at all. Since your child will have earned income, he or she could open an RRSP and would be eligible to contribute, even when under 18 years of age. Your allowance would allow your child to invest his or her earnings in an RRSP.

What We Have Learned:
- *investing cash receipts in the right hands is effectively income-splitting.*
- *invest child tax benefits in your child's name.*
- *the higher-income spouse should pay household expenses.*
- *invest inheritances in the right name.*
- *give a working child an allowance.*

LESSON 31

Take advantage of statutory provisions in the Income Tax Act to split income.

$ | $

The Income Tax Act (the Act) itself provides opportunities for income-splitting in a few situations that may apply to you at some point. Five such opportunities are detailed here.

22. SPLIT TAX ON CPP BENEFITS WITH YOUR SPOUSE. The Act allows you to take up to fifty percent of your CPP benefits received and to report the income on your spouse's return. The deal is reciprocal, meaning that the same proportion of your spouse's CPP benefits must be included on your tax return. Where you have received more CPP benefits than your spouse and your annual income is higher, it makes good sense to split the income in this way. For example, if your CPP benefits were $7,000 in the year, and your spouse had no income at all, your spouse could report $3,500 on his or her tax return and save you $1,750 in taxes where your marginal tax rate is 50%. A formal request must be made to Human Resources Development Canada (formerly Health and Welfare Canada) to make arrangements for this split of CPP benefits.

23. CONTRIBUTE TO A SPOUSAL RRSP. You're able to contribute to an RRSP under which your spouse is the annuitant. Note that this is different than giving your spouse funds to contribute to his or her own RRSP – a special spousal plan needs to be set up where you're the contributor and your spouse is the annuitant. When the funds are distributed upon retirement they will be taxed in your spouse's hands. There are special rules regarding withdrawals which we'll talk more about in lesson 72.

24. CONTRIBUTE TO AN RESP. A Registered Education Savings Plan (RESP) works similar to a spousal RRSP. Although there's no deduction permitted for contributions to an RESP, the income earned in the plan will grow tax-free until the funds are withdrawn to pay for your child's education. At that time, the income portion of the withdrawal is taxed in your child's hands at a lower marginal tax rate. There are some important rules to consider before contributing to an RESP, and we'll talk more about these in lesson 33, point 2.

25. TRANSFER DIVIDEND INCOME TO YOUR SPOUSE. If your spouse's income is fairly low, and he or she has earned dividends, you might consider moving the dividends to your tax return. Although it may sound strange to put dividends on the return of the higher-income spouse, there are situations where it may actually save you money. You're permitted to make this transfer of dividends only where the switch will increase the spousal credit you're claiming, and with the dividend tax credit your taxes will actually be reduced if your taxable income is in the lowest bracket (that is, below $29,590). Where your income is above $29,590 this switch is generally not worth doing.

26. PAY YOUR SPOUSE ALIMONY AND MAINTENANCE. The type of fuss that's required to implement this income-splitting idea generally goes beyond what the average family will do to save taxes. But, if you happen to find yourself in a situation where you're required to pay alimony and maintenance, the government will openly allow you to move income from your return to your spouse's simply by putting the amount in writing. Not surprisingly, there are few taxpayers who are motivated to maximize this transfer to split income.

What We Have Learned:
- *the Income Tax Act itself provides opportunities for income-splitting in a few situations.*
- *split tax on CPP benefits with your spouse.*
- *contribute to a spousal RRSP.*
- *contribute to an RESP.*
- *transfer dividend income to your spouse.*
- *pay your spouse alimony and maintenance.*

LESSON 32

Use a business or corporation to split income.

When you run your own business, whether it's through a corporation or as a proprietorship or partnership, new opportunities for income-splitting can be found. Here are a few ideas.

27. PAY FAMILY MEMBERS A SALARY. When you own a business and a family member helps out in some way, you can pay him or her a reasonable salary. This puts income in your spouse's hands and takes it out of your hands by way of a deduction for the business. This remains one of the more common ways to split income.

28. ENTER INTO A BUSINESS PARTNERSHIP WITH FAMILY. A partnership does not pay taxes, rather it passes the profits to the individual partners to be taxed in their hands. When two people are partners in a business, the profits of the business are split in accordance with the partnership agreement. When running a business, consider operating in a partnership with your spouse or child to effectively split income by taxing a portion of the profits in their hands. A written partnership agreement identifying the split of profits, among other things, is a necessity.

29. COMPLETE AN ESTATE FREEZE. This idea is common among business owners who operate through a corporation. In a nutshell, as a shareholder you should consider exchanging the common shares you own for new preferred shares where your common shares are worth more than what you paid for them. The new preferred shares you receive will have the same value as the common shares, but the value will be fixed and will not increase over time. Your child can now purchase common shares in the company for a nominal amount. The future growth in the company will accrue to your child's shares, not yours, so that you have effectively moved income into his or her hands. Generally, you won't undertake an estate freeze early in your career – you'll want to wait until the shares you own have increased substantially in value. An estate freeze not only permits income-splitting, but accomplishes many other important planning ideas such as permanently fixing your tax liability upon death so that you know today what you will owe. An estate freeze does not mean giving up control of the company or cutting yourself off from dividends and other income – visit your tax professional to discuss it.

30. USE TWO CORPORATIONS TO GIVE MONEY TO YOUR SPOUSE. The objective here is to get money from your hands into your lower-income spouse's hands to be invested and taxed at a lower rate. The attribution rules only apply when an individual lends money to another individual or to a corporation. Loans between corporations are not caught under the rules. Where you and your spouse each have a corporation, you can advance funds to your company who can in turn make a loan to your spouse's corporation. Your spouse's corporation can then invest the money and pay dividends out to your spouse. The dividends will be taxable to your spouse, but he or she can receive up to $23,760 in dividends without paying a cent in tax provided it's your spouse's only source of income. This is due to the dividend tax credit available. Where your spouse has other income, the amount of the dividend that can be paid tax-free will be reduced, but may still be substantial. Once the dividend is paid out, the money is your spouse's, and he or she is free to invest it at a lower tax rate.

31. OWN A CORPORATION WITH YOUR SPOUSE. Another way of putting cash in your lower-income spouse's hands is to own a corporation with him or her. It has to be done correctly. You'll need to own 91% or more of the company while your spouse will own the remaining shares. In addition, the shares you hold must be a different class of shares than your spouse's. You can advance funds to the company for it to invest and the company can pay dividends on the class of shares held by your spouse. With no other income, your spouse can receive up to $23,760 in dividends tax-free from the company to invest and be taxed at a lower rate. Be sure to visit a tax professional if you implement this idea.

What We Have Learned:
- *using a business or corporation can provide additional ways to split income.*
- *pay family members a salary.*
- *enter into a business partnership with family.*
- *complete an estate freeze.*
- *use two corporations to give money to your spouse.*
- *own a corporation with your spouse.*

One more thought

Some of the ideas presented here are aggressive. They are all within the letter of the law, however Revenue Canada may not appreciate their use. If you're considering use of the more aggressive ideas, be sure to visit your tax professional to be advised of any drawbacks. Generally, you will not risk losing anything by implementing the ideas since any attributed income would have been taxed in your hands anyway.

Deferring Taxable Income

5

When we speak of deferring taxable income we're talking about earning income today, but paying tax on it tomorrow. So what if we defer the tax – we're still going to pay it, right? Sure, but paying a dollar in tax today is not the same as paying a dollar in tax tomorrow. Think back to our talk in chapter 2 about the time value of money (lesson 4) – the concept is important here. If you're able to postpone the payment of tax, those dollars can be used for other things – perhaps investments. If you can defer the tax long enough, the tax could very well be paid using the income you earn on the investments.

Suppose you owe $100 in taxes, but instead of paying this year, you're able to defer the payment for one year. Is your true tax liability $100? The answer is no. Since a dollar today is worth more than a dollar tomorrow, paying in tomorrow's dollars will actually cost you less.

Bart's Deferral

Bart owes Revenue Canada $100 in taxes, but he managed to defer payment of this liability for one year. So now Bart owes Revenue Canada $100 one year from now. Bart now takes $91 and sets it aside for one year. Over the year he earns 10% on his money and ends up with $100 one year from now. He then uses the $100 to pay his taxes. The true cost to Bart was not $100, but just $91. By deferring his taxes for one year he saved almost 10% of his tax liability.

The amount saved by deferring your taxes will depend on the rate of return you can earn between now and the time you have to make your tax payment. The chart below shows your true cost of a $100 tax liability at different rates of return for different deferral times. For example, if you owe $100 but can defer payment for ten years, and you can earn 9% on your money between now and then, your true cost is only $42.

Rate of Return (%)	True Cost of $100 in Taxes Paid in the Future			
	1yr	3yrs	5yrs	10yrs
5	$ 95	$ 86	$ 78	$ 61
7	93	82	71	51
9	92	77	65	42
11	90	73	59	35
13	88	69	54	29
15	87	66	50	25
17	85	62	46	21
19	84	59	42	18
21	83	56	39	15
23	81	54	36	13

There are a few ways you can defer payment of taxes. Some are easier than others, and some combine deferring income with splitting or reducing income. The lessons that follow reflect some of the best ideas available.

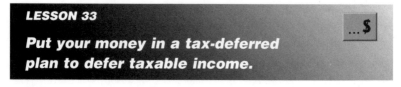

LESSON 33

Put your money in a tax-deferred plan to defer taxable income.

A tax-deferred plan will allow you to invest money in such a way that it grows on a tax-free basis until you take the money out of the plan, at which time you're taxed on it. Often, your marginal tax rate in the year you take the money out of the plan will be lower than when you put it in, so you have not only deferred taxes, but you have actually reduced your tax bill at the same time. The following ideas deal with tax-deferred plans.

1. CONTRIBUTE TO AN RRSP. A Registered Retirement Savings Plan (RRSP) is the most common tool used to defer taxes. Your money will grow inside your RRSP on a tax-free basis and will only be taxed when you withdraw the funds, so you're deferring tax on the income earned inside the plan. But there's more. Since you get a deduction for contributing to your RRSP you not only defer tax on the income accruing inside the plan, but on the income contributed to the plan. In the year you reach age 71 you should consider rolling your RRSP funds into a Registered Retirement Income Fund (RRIF), a Life Income Fund (LIF), or purchasing a life annuity, all of which will defer taxes even longer. In chapter 7 we'll look at RRSPs in much more detail, although we mention them here first because they offer the best deferral, are available to all Canadians, and can be used to defer any dollar amount.

2. CONTRIBUTE TO AN RESP. We introduced Registered Education Savings Plans (RESPs) briefly in lesson 31, point 24. An RESP is a plan to which you can make contributions for a child's or grand-child's education. There's a deferral of tax since the money grows tax-free until the student makes a withdrawal to attend school, at which time the accumulated income is taxed in the child's hands. The student may not pay any tax on the withdrawal if his income is low enough. There's no deduction for you when you make a contribution. Contributions to an RESP cannot exceed $1,500 for each child in each calendar year, and there's an overall limit of $31,500 per child over the life of the plan.

One caution: if your child fails to attend a qualifying educational institution later in life, you'll be able to get back the amount of your contributions, but not the income that had accrued in the plan over the years. Some plans offer flexibility in terms of who the beneficiary can be (some plans even allow the beneficiary to be changed to the contributor – you), but ask some questions before investing in an RESP.

3. TAKE PART IN YOUR COMPANY'S RPP. If your employer has a Registered Pension Plan (RPP) you may want to take part in it. Much like an RRSP contribution, you receive a deduction for contributions to such a plan. In addition, most RPPs provide for your employer to make contributions on your behalf which might result in more retirement savings than you could accomplish yourself. The money in your RPP will grow tax-free and you'll be taxed when you receive payments out of the plan. If you take part in an RPP your contributions to an RRSP will be limited by a *pension adjustment* so that you don't receive an unfair advantage over others who may not have the opportunity to be part of an RPP.

4. TAKE PART IN A DPSP. Your employer may offer a Deferred Profit Sharing Plan (DPSP) to its employees. Employees do not contribute to a DPSP – it's entirely funded by the employer who is able to make contributions for each employee up to a certain limit, generally 18% of your income or $6,750 for 1996 ($7,250 for 1997, $7,750 for 1998, and indexed thereafter) whichever is less. Contributions must be made based on the company's profits, and so no contributions need to made in years the company loses money. Amounts inside a DPSP grow tax-free until they're paid out to you. A portion of your payments from a DPSP may be tax-free if they represent your pre-1991 contributions when employees were allowed to contribute to DPSPs. Further, most plans provide that taxable amounts can be paid out to you over a ten year period (maximum) which results in a further deferral. Finally, you might consider rolling the proceeds into a term-certain annuity (not exceeding 15 years), or into an RRSP or RPP to defer tax even longer.

5. NEGOTIATE AN RCA. A Retirement Compensation Arrangement (RCA) is basically an unregistered pension plan. Contributions are generally made by your employer although you can contribute to an RCA as well. Your contributions for 1989 and later years will be deductible provided the RCA is governed by a Canadian custodian, the contributions are required under the terms of your employment, and the contributions don't exceed your employer's contributions. RCA contributions will affect the amount you can contribute to your RRSP. You will not pay tax on amounts contributed to the plan by your employer until you actually receive the cash. Your employer, however, will pay a 50% tax on contributions which will be refunded to the company once the amounts are paid out to you.

6. ROLLOVER A RETIRING ALLOWANCE. A retiring allowance is an amount received by you (or a relative after your death) on or after your retirement in recognition of long service, including early retirement incentives or other payments in respect of a loss of employment, whether or not the amount was received as a termination payment or damages from loss of office. It's important that the allowance not be salary in disguise. Where you have received such a payment you can roll it into an RRSP or RPP to defer tax on the payment. The maximum that can be rolled into your RRSP or RPP is $2,000 for each year (or portion of a calendar year) of your employment up to and including 1995, plus an additional $1,500 for each year before 1989 that you were employed by the same employer and for which your employer's contributions to an RPP or DPSP had not vested. It could be to your advantage to use your retiring allowance as a bargaining tool at the time of loss of employment. A point to watch for is an Alternative Minimum Tax (AMT) problem, however AMT, if paid, can be recovered within the following seven tax years (more about the AMT in lesson 118). Unfortunately, no amount with respect to employment in 1996 and later years is eligible for a tax-free rollover thanks to changes introduced in the February 1995 federal budget – see more in lesson 64.

7. BEWARE OF SDAs, THEY DON'T USUALLY WORK. If you're not careful, you might try to defer taxable income but end up being taxed on amounts you have not even received yet. The rules were introduced back in 1986 when the term Salary Deferral Arrangement (SDA) became part of the Act. An SDA is an arrangement between you and your employer where you have postponed the receipt of a portion of your compensation, mainly for the purpose of deferring taxable income. Where you have such an arrangement, the rules require that you include in income any of the amounts deferred. Further, where the deferred compensation is earning interest or other amounts, that income will be taxable to you in the year it's earned. Not all the news is bad though. There are some exceptions to the rule, which brings us to points 8 and 9.

8. NEGOTIATE A LEAVE OF ABSENCE OR SABBATICAL PLAN. One exception to the SDA problem noted previously is when you are involved in a leave of absence or sabbatical plan. These plans will avoid the SDA problems if they provide for deferrals of not more than 6 years, and for a deferral of not more than one third of your salary for a leave. The leave must commence not later than the seventh year and must be at least six months (or three months where the leave is to allow your full-time attendance at an educational institution). The plan must provide for you to return to work for at least as long as the leave and must pay deferred amounts in the seventh year whether or not you actually take a leave. This is a standard feature of most teaching contracts and is becoming more common in other industries.

9. ARRANGE TO DEFER A BONUS FOR THREE YEARS. Another exception to the SDA problem noted in point 7 is the deferral of a bonus for three years. Where you have the right to receive a bonus for work done in a particular year, payment of that bonus can be deferred for up to three years without fear of being taxed until you receive the cash. For example, if your employer grants you the right to a bonus for work that you did in 1996, your employer can defer payment of that bonus until December 31st 1999, although payment must be made on or before that date. You won't be taxed on the bonus until the year you actually receive it.

10. ESTABLISH AN IPP. An Individual Pension Plan (IPP) is a defined benefit pension plan specifically tailored for one shareholder or senior executive. An IPP will allow you to increase your annual deductible contributions for retirement. In fact, contributions can be higher for you where an IPP is used than could be made under the RRSP contribution limits. For example, contribution levels for a 45 year old male in 1996 and 1997 could be as high as $18,100 under an IPP compared to $13,500 under an RRSP. The potential benefit in this example is about $263,465 of additional income at retirement assuming 20 years of compounding at 10%. Generally, an IPP is best for someone who is 45 to 50 years of age. There will be some significant costs associated with setting up and administering an IPP, including a tri-annual actuarial valuation, but the benefits may outweigh these costs.

11. INVEST IN AN EXEMPT INSURANCE POLICY. Buying insurance can be an intimidating experience since many people don't truly understand the differences among the many products available. Exempt policies offer the best of two worlds – insurance plus investments. They are a special product from a tax point of view because the investment portion grows tax-free. The type of investments held in the policy can vary depending on your preference. Because of the tax-free compounding you effectively defer tax until you either fully or partially surrender the policy, or borrow from the accumulated investments. If you hold onto the policy until your death, your beneficiaries receive the benefits tax-free. More about this in lesson 125.

12. INVEST IN A PRESCRIBED TERM-CERTAIN ANNUITY. A prescribed term-certain annuity can provide a deferral of tax in its early years. It works this way: you buy an annuity that promises to make monthly payments to you for a fixed period of time (they can start at three years and run to age 90). The annuity pays a rate of interest that is fixed at the start. Each payment is a blend of interest and a return of your capital. Normally, in the early years of an annuity, the majority of each payment is actually interest while a small portion is a return of your capital. It's not until later in the annuity's life that most of your capital is returned to you. As a result, you'd expect a large portion of your early annuity payments to be taxable (since they are mostly interest).

A prescribed term annuity will defer taxable income because it will pay back your capital equally over the life of the annuity, meaning that a smaller portion of your payments received will be taxable in the early years. Conversely, you will pay a little more tax in the later years of the annuity than you would normally expect, but if you're in a lower tax bracket in those years, your tax savings can be significant. Prescribed term-certain annuities can provide a tax deferral that other investments, like GICs, cannot.

What We Have Learned:
- *a tax-deferred plan allows money to grow tax-free until it's withdrawn.*
- *contribute to an RRSP.*
- *contribute to an RESP.*
- *take part in your company's RPP.*
- *take part in a DPSP.*
- *negotiate an RCA.*
- *rollover a retiring allowance.*
- *beware of SDAs, they don't usually work.*
- *negotiate a leave of absence or sabbatical plan.*
- *arrange to defer a bonus for three years.*

- *establish an IPP.*
- *invest in an exempt insurance policy.*
- *invest in a prescribed term-certain annuity.*

LESSON 34

Control the timing of your interest, dividends, and capital gains to defer taxable income.

...$

In certain situations you'll be able to choose the year in which you report interest, dividends, and capital gains. The idea is to put off reporting these amounts as income for as long as possible.

13. ONLY REPORT INTEREST EVERY THREE YEARS WHERE POSSIBLE. For investment contracts acquired before 1990, the *three-year accrual rule* allows you to defer reporting interest income where it has been earned but not yet received by you. The rule requires that all interest earned, but not yet received, be included in income every three years, unless previously reported. Investments purchased in 1990 or later are subject to the *annual accrual rule* where you must report income every year, whether received or not. The issuers of such investments are required to provide you with a T5 slip each year.

14. BUY CAPITAL PROPERTY AND TIME ITS SALE. Capital property is pretty much anything you buy that could appreciate in value so that you end up selling it at a profit. This includes stocks, bonds, mutual funds, real estate, artwork, among other things. A sure way to defer taxable income and taxes is to invest in capital property that will appreciate in value. You defer taxes because you will not be taxed on any gains until you dispose of the property. So, your mutual funds might earn an average annual return of 20% over the next five or ten years, and you might pay very little tax until you dispose of them. Which brings us to the next point: you can defer tax on capital gains by disposing of your capital property after the end of the year, rather than before year end.

David Dumps Chagall

Our client David owned an original painting by Chagall that cost him $23,000 but was worth $40,000 (because Chagall had died) when he decided he needed the money more than the painting. He found a buyer in November of last year, but arranged for the sale to take place on January 1st of this year. By doing this, he deferred the capital gain, and tax, by one full year. His tax liability of $6,500 really only cost him $5,900 (due to the time value of money) since he deferred the payment for one year.

15. CLAIM A CAPITAL GAINS RESERVE. Where you've sold capital property for a gain and you've agreed to take payment in instalments over time, you'll be able to claim a reserve (a deduction) each year for the portion of the proceeds that you have not yet collected. This means that the gain on your sale will be taxed as income over a number of years, rather than reporting the entire gain in the year of the sale. The rules work so that you'll be able to defer tax on the gain for up to five years, so by the time five years has passed, you will have been taxed on the full gain. A clever idea would be to structure your sale so that you receive instalments over a five year period. This works especially well where you expect your marginal tax rate to drop over the next five years, since part of the gain would be taxed at a lower rate. See lesson 48 for an additional idea if you're going to try this.

16. INVEST IN A SECTOR PROGRAM. Canadian International (C.I.) Group is a mutual fund company that offers investors many different mutual funds to choose from. C.I. offers the *Sector Program* which will allow you to hold many of C.I.'s funds and to switch between the funds on a tax-free basis. Normally, switching from one fund to another will constitute a disposition, and will result in a taxable capital gain where the fund has increased in value since buying it. In the Sector Program, your money is used to purchase units in the C.I. Sector Fund, and these units are then used to invest in units of the individual C.I. mutual funds. You'll be able to exchange units of one fund with those of another fund based on current market values without triggering a disposition for tax purposes. You'll only pay tax on gains when you dispose of your Sector Fund units. In effect, you're able to realize capital gains without paying tax until a later date. You'll be able to defer tax as long as you hold onto your Sector Fund units.

For example, if you invest $10,000 in the Sector Fund for 20 years, earn 10% capital appreciation each year, and rotate (switch) your investments each year, you'll end up with $67,275 and will not pay tax on the gain until you sell your Sector Fund units. If you had been invested in another mutual fund and were taxed on your gains from switching each year, you would have just $32,071 over the same period. You're able to more than double your investment by deferring tax on your gains. AGF and GT Global are other mutual fund companies offering this type of program, and others are sure to follow soon, just ask an investment broker.

17. INVEST IN TAX-DEFERRED PREFERRED SHARES. For those of you who have been around long enough to remember the tax-deferred preferred shares (TDPS) of 1978 that effectively allowed investors to have dividends taxed as capital gains, don't be confused, we're talking about something entirely different here! We won't get into a discussion about those TDPS from 1978 because they're no longer with us. Let's talk about a new type of TDPS. The TDPSs we're introducing to you work this way: you buy the preferred shares at a fixed purchase price. The shares become redeemable by the issuing company several years down the road for a pre-determined higher price. The difference between your purchase price and the redemption price is taxed in your hands as a dividend.

This TDPS is really nothing more than a bond in disguise. Think about it. A bond is purchased at a certain price and matures at a pre-determined price. The only difference is that a bond earns interest income which is *payable* annually (whether it is actually *paid* annually is a different issue), and consequently taxed each year. With the TDPS, the redemption price is not actually payable to you until the pre-determined redemption date, and so tax is deferred until that time. There are very few of these TDPSs available currently, but they're a great idea for those investing outside their RRSPs since you can enjoy some of the tax deferral normally enjoyed inside your RRSP. See more information in lesson 121.

What We Have Learned:
- *postpone the reporting of interest, dividends, and capital gains for as long as possible.*
- *only report interest every three years where possible.*
- *buy capital property and time its sale.*
- *claim a capital gains reserve.*
- *invest in a sector program.*
- *invest in tax-deferred preferred shares.*

LESSON 35

Use your business or corporation to defer taxable income.

...$

As with splitting taxable income, the opportunities to defer taxable income are increased when you own an unincorporated or incorporated business.

18. INCORPORATE YOUR BUSINESS. This idea makes sense once your business has become profitable. The amount of income tax paid by a Canadian Controlled Private Corporation (CCPC) will be between 18% and 23%, depending on your province. This rate could be considerably lower than your own marginal tax rate. If so, it makes sense to pay tax in the company and defer the timing of payouts from the corporation to you. By doing this, you pay tax at, say, 23% rather than your marginal rate of, perhaps, 40% resulting in a deferral of 17% of the taxes you otherwise would have paid.

Thomas Incorporates

Thomas's plumbing business has been doing well for the past couple of years. Last year we recommended that he incorporate his business, so he did. He earned net income of $75,000 last year and paid tax in the corporation of $17,130. He would have paid taxes of $27,210 had he earned the income personally. The difference amounts to $10,080 which is cash that he plowed back into his business – in effect, the government has invested $10,080 in Thomas's business with no strings attached. Theoretically, he'll pay the difference to the taxman when the company pays him dividends, but in actual fact, he may experience some permanent tax savings.

19. CHOOSE THE RIGHT YEAR END FOR YOUR UNINCORPORATED BUSINESS. The benefit available by choosing the proper year end for your unincorporated business has been largely reduced by changes in the 1995 federal budget and subsequent technical amendments. The good news is that there's still the possibility to defer taxable income and taxes.

THE WAY IT WAS

It used to be that you could defer taxes for one full year by choosing a January 31st year end. For example, if your unincorporated business earned $40,000 for the year ended January 31, 1994, you were not required to include the $40,000 in your personal income until you filed your 1994 tax return on April 30, 1995. A full one year deferral. The government decided to put a stop to this type of benefit.

THE WAY IT IS NOW

Beginning with the 1995 tax year you have two choices to pick from: (1) adopt a December 31st year end, or (2) keep your non-calendar year end and make required adjustments to your income. The calculations involved in either case are complicated, so we won't bore you with them here. Let's look at the basics though.

• ADOPT A DECEMBER 31ST YEAR END:

Suppose you've always had a January 31st year end and now want to switch to a calendar year end in 1995. You'll have a "stub period" from February 1 to December 31, 1995. You'll be able to report your income for the stub period little by little over the next ten years. Good thing, otherwise you'd get hit with 11 extra months of income in 1995 and the stub period would hurt a lot more than any stubbed toe ever could. Note that once you've switched to a December 31st year end, there's no changing again after that.

• KEEP YOUR NON-CALENDAR YEAR END:

If you keep a non-calendar year end you'll be required each year to prepay taxes to cover each year's stub period. The prepayment is an estimate based on a fraction of your current year's income. So, if your year end is January 31st, you would prepay taxes on 11/12ths of your January 31st income, which is considered by the taxman to be an estimate of taxes owing for the stub period income. In the following year you would compare the prepaid amount with the actual amount owing and make an adjustment to your income. Then you would add the prepaid amount for the next year. Lost yet? If not – good for you. Otherwise, keep in mind our rule of thumb.

• OUR RULE OF THUMB:

Maintain a non-calendar year end only when you are confident that your business income will rise consistently in the future, or where there are strong business (aside from tax) reasons for doing so.

This rule makes sense because you'll be prepaying tax based on the current year's income level. Where income is expected to rise next year, the prepayment will be less than the actual amount of taxes owing. The result is that you have deferred taxes. The amount of tax deferred is the difference between the prepaid amount and the actual taxes owing. Where your income is consistently rising, you'll defer taxes until the next year that your income drops, at which time you'll get hit with the tax you managed to defer earlier, but remember: taxes tomorrow will cost you less than the same taxes paid today.

Finally, where your income falls in the future and you have maintained your non-calendar year end, you will have prepaid more than your actual taxes, and you have not deferred anything – in fact, you'll be worse off. That's the time you'll want to move to a December 31st year end – something you can do in any future year – be sure to consult your tax professional. Where you're just starting a new business, there will be no point in choosing a non-calendar year end since you'll prepay taxes for the stub period between your year end and December 31st – that is, you'll pay tax on income you haven't earned yet with no relief of any kind.

20. TAKE A SHAREHOLDER LOAN. If, as a shareholder, you borrow money from your company, the amount will be included in your income if it's not repaid by the end of the company's following tax year. You could defer paying tax for two years.

Cary's Loan
Cary owns shares in the family corporation. The company has a December 31st year end. On January 1, 1996 the company loaned Cary $10,000. Since the loan was not repaid by December 31, 1997, Cary was required to include the amount in his income for his 1996 tax year. He had to amend his 1996 return to make the change, and he paid some interest since the tax on the $10,000 income was really due on April 30, 1997 when he filed his 1996 tax return. The interest owing, however, was much less than the income he earned while he invested the $10,000 from January 1, 1996 to December 31, 1997, a two year period.

There are certain shareholder loans that may be excluded from the rule that includes the loan in income. For example, the following loans will not necessarily be included in your income where the loan is made in your capacity as an employee (not a shareholder) and bona fide arrangements for repayment are made: a loan used to acquire a home, to acquire shares from the treasury of the company, or to acquire a vehicle for use in the course of your employment. Note also that this income inclusion rule won't apply where you own less than 10% of any class of shares that have been issued to you (the loan must still be in your capacity as an employee and bona fide arrangements for repayment must exist), or where you fully repay the loan within one year after the end of the company's tax year in which the loan was outstanding. See lesson 26 for more details.

21. POSTPONE DIVIDENDS UNTIL AFTER YEAR END. Where you're a shareholder in a private company you'll often have influence over the timing of dividends. Much like our example above for capital property, you'll be better off having the company pay you a dividend on January 1st of next year than December 31st of this year. This postpones, for a full year, the requirement to report the dividend and pay tax on it. In addition, there are no requirements for the company to withhold income taxes, UIC, or CPP on dividends paid to you. There may be situations where it's advantageous for the dividends to be paid sooner rather than later – when the dividends are tax-free, for example, but in many cases you'll be better off by deferring them. Everyone's situation is different, so see your tax professional.

22. PAY A BONUS AFTER YEAR END. When your corporation declares a bonus at year end, it has 180 days to make the payment to you before it becomes non-deductible by the company. This means that your company that has a December 31st year end can declare a bonus on December 31, 1996 and withhold payment until June 29, 1997. The benefit is that the company gets a deduction on December 31, 1996, but you won't pay tax for another six months until the bonus is paid to you and withholding taxes are remitted to the government (withholding taxes remitted to the taxman serve as proof that your bonus was paid within the 180 day limit). If, for example, your company declares a $10,000 bonus on December 31, 1996 it would save $2,200 today while you might owe $2,200 6 months later *if your marginal tax rate is similar to the company's.* The benefit is the income you could earn on the $2,200 in that 6 month period, less taxes on that income of course. Check your marginal tax rate to see if this idea is a good one for you.

23. CLAIM AN INCOME RESERVE. There are times when your business might make a sale to a customer or client with an agreement that you'll be paid over time. Where you've earned business income, you'll be able to take a deduction (reserve) for a portion of the income where two conditions are met: (1) a portion of the sale amount is not due until after the business's year end, and (2) at least a part of the sale amount was, at the time of the sale, not due for another two years. When these conditions are met, you'll be able to take the sale amount into income over a maximum three year period. You may want to structure a sale to take advantage of the deferral that's available under these rules. The downside, of course, is that you won't collect some of your money for another three years. Try charging interest on the outstanding balance to make this idea worth your while.

24. USE A FOREIGN CORPORATION. When you earn investment income inside a foreign corporation you may be able to defer tax for a full year. Here's how it works: set up a corporation in a tax haven (so that any income inside the corporation will not be taxed in that jurisdiction) and put money into the corporation for investment purposes. The *foreign accrual property income (FAPI) rules* in Canada will require you to report the company's investment income on your own personal tax return, but deferral for a full year is possible because the amount included in your personal income will be the investment income for the company's tax year ending in your personal tax year. Here's an example.

Tim's Tax Haven
Tim set up a corporation in 1996 in the Cayman Islands and loaned $100,000 to the company. Tim chose January 31st as the company's year end. In the year ended January 31, 1997 (the first year end of the company), the company earned $15,000 in investment income. Tim will have to include the $15,000 in his personal income because of the FAPI rules. He'll include the amount as income on his 1997 personal tax return because the money was earned by the company in its 1997 year (the year ended January 31, 1997). This means that income earned by the company in its year ended January 31, 1997 will not be taxed until April 30, 1998 – a deferral of one full year. The company itself won't pay any taxes since it resides in a jurisdiction where there is no tax.

You'll have to watch for the requirement to pay quarterly tax instalments where you're consistently reporting additional income on your personal tax return. This could reduce your deferral time after the first year – see lesson 105.

There's more good news if you're looking to defer taxable income using a foreign corporation. In a situation where you do not control the corporation (the definition of *control* is complex here) or where the corporation earns active business income you may be able to defer tax indefinitely by leaving the income in the corporation. You'll only be taxed when the corporation pays the income out to you as dividends. Be sure to visit a tax professional to ensure you structure your affairs properly if you want to take advantage of this indefinite deferral.

What We Have Learned:
- *a business will increase your opportunities to defer taxable income.*
- *incorporate your business.*
- *choose the right year end for your unincorporated business.*
- *take a shareholder loan.*
- *postpone dividends until after year end.*
- *pay a bonus after year end.*
- *claim an income reserve.*
- *use a foreign corporation.*

Converting Taxable Income

What Is Conversion?

Which would you rather own, a GIC or preferred shares in ABC company? Maybe you'd prefer to own common shares, or perhaps a government bond. There are a number of things to consider before choosing any particular investment, and we'll talk more about this in chapter 9. For now, it's important to realize that one factor which should affect your investment decisions is the amount of tax you'll pay on your investment earnings. By no means make your decision for tax reasons alone, but don't make the mistake of ignoring taxes, because different investments will attract different marginal rates of tax depending on the type of income earned. The types of income are: interest, dividends, and capital gains.

We want to introduce the concept of converting taxable income. We're talking about converting your income from one *type* that attracts a high rate of tax to a different type that attracts a lower rate of tax.

Connie's Conversion

Connie is a client of ours who recently inherited $10,000. She invested the money in a 7.5% GIC which paid her $750 in interest last year. She paid taxes of $400 on the interest income, and was left with $350 in her pocket. We told her to convert her interest income into dividends by investing in preferred shares of ABC company paying an annual dividend of 6.0%.

She didn't like the idea because her 7.5% GIC pays more than a 6.0% preferred share. Think about your after-tax income we told her. This year, she received $600 in dividends on those ABC preferred shares and paid taxes of $200. She was left with $400 in her pocket. She ended up with $50 more in her pocket this year because her 6.0% dividend was not taxed as highly as her 7.5% interest income. Connie successfully converted her taxable income.

The moral of the story? Dividends are taxed at a lower marginal rate than interest income. In fact, there's a difference in the marginal tax rate on all three types of investment income.

LESSON 36

$▸$

Dividends are taxed at a lower rate than capital gains, which are taxed at a lower rate than interest.

The interesting thing is, no matter which province you live in, dividends are taxed at a lower rate than capital gains which are taxed at a lower rate than interest. Refer to Appendix 2 at the back of the book for a breakdown of marginal tax rates on each type of income. You'll notice, for example, that in Ontario, if you're in the highest tax bracket, you'll pay taxes at 53.2% on interest, 39.9% on capital gains, and just 35.9% on dividends in 1996.

What We Have Learned:
- *there are different marginal tax rates on each type of investment income: interest, dividends, and capital gains.*
- *dividends are taxed at a lower rate than capital gains which are taxed at a lower rate than interest.*
- *this is true in every province.*

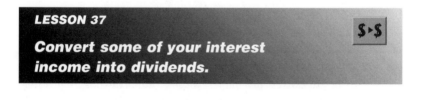

LESSON 37

$▸$

Convert some of your interest income into dividends.

So it follows that if dividends are taxed less than interest, we should all be earning dividends instead, right? Partly right. Don't forget, taxes are only one consideration when deciding what to invest in. To earn dividends you have to invest in common or preferred shares (or mutual funds that do so). Common and preferred shares may have more risk attached to them than the GICs you're currently invested in. The key word in this lesson is *some*. Convert *some* of your interest into dividends. Exactly how much will depend on other factors like your age and risk tolerance. As a bonus, investing in common shares (and some preferred shares) will offer the potential for capital gains (or losses) which are also taxed at a much lower rate than interest.

For every $100 in dividends that you earn, you'll have to earn $130 in interest, on average, to end up with the same money in your pocket after taxes. So, as a rule of thumb you'll need to earn 1.3 times more in interest to be in the same position, after-taxes, as earning dividends. For example, if you can earn a 5% rate of return by way of dividends, you had better be able to earn 6.5% (5% x 1.3) in interest to end up with the same money in your hands after taxes.

What We Have Learned:
- *don't convert __all__ but convert __some__ of your interest into dividends.*
- *you must invest in common or preferred shares (or mutual funds that do so) to earn dividends; these also offer the potential for capital gains which are taxed favourably.*
- *you'll need to earn interest income equal to 1.3 times your dividend income to end up with the same money in your pockets after taxes.*

LESSON 38

$▸$

Using your capital gains exemption means capital gains are best.

There was once a day when capital gains were even better than dividends when it came to saving tax dollars. This was due to the $100,000 lifetime capital gains exemption that was available to shelter your capital gains from tax. The capital gains exemption is neither gone nor forgotten – not yet anyway. Although your last chance to claim the exemption was on your 1994 tax return, you can still amend that return and claim the exemption on gains that accrued up to February 22, 1994. In addition, there's a $500,000 exemption still available to shelter gains on the shares of qualifying small business corporations and on operating farms. See lesson 16 for more details. If you happen to be able to use your capital gains exemption, your rate of tax on that gain will be nil, which is even better than the rate on dividends.

What We Have Learned:

- *using your capital gains exemption will result in lower taxes on capital gains than on dividends.*
- *the $100,000 lifetime capital gains exemption is still available if you amend your 1994 tax return.*
- *a $500,000 exemption is also available to owners of shares in qualifying small business corporations and farms.*
- *see lesson 16 for more details.*

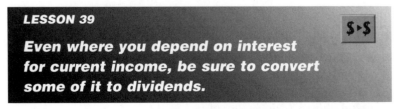

LESSON 39

Even where you depend on interest for current income, be sure to convert some of it to dividends.

Many of our clients rely on interest-bearing investments to provide them with income for daily living. Retirees are often in this boat. The temptation for most of these clients has been to keep all their funds tied up in GICs, treasury bills, or other safe investments. The argument is that by putting money into conservative, safe investments there's no risk of losing anything, and so there will always be capital there to provide income.

While it's true that certain people should be investing in conservative, safe investments, it's also true that you can earn dividends while doing so. Certain preferred shares, for example, can be very safe and will meet your objective of preserving capital. This being the case, it makes sense to search out shares to invest in to convert some of that interest into dividends. Make a trip to an investment broker for help. Your pocket book will thank you.

What We Have Learned:
- *some people rely on interest-bearing investments to provide income for daily living.*
- *the temptation is to keep all your money in safe interest-bearing investments to preserve capital.*
- *certain preferred shares will meet your objective of preserving capital since they too are very safe.*
- *search out shares to invest in to convert some of your interest into dividends.*

LESSON 40
Dividends and capital gains earned inside your RRSP lose their identity.

$▸$

We like to call this *investment amnesia*. Any income you earn inside your RRSP, whether it's interest, dividends, or capital gains, is going to be taxed as regular income when it's withdrawn. Regular income is taxed at the same marginal rate as interest income. In effect, dividends and capital gains lose their identity when earned inside your RRSP.

Is this a bad thing? Does this mean you should avoid dividends and capital gains inside your RRSP? The answer is no! The objective for your RRSP is simple: maximize your investment returns. It just so happens that investing some of your money in shares that pay dividends and capital gains has time and time again offered superior returns, over the long run, than investing in interest-bearing investments alone. So don't worry about investment amnesia when it comes to your RRSP. One fact remains though, if you're investing money outside your RRSP, then be sure to convert some of your interest to dividends to reduce your tax exposure.

What We Have Learned:
- *dividends and capital gains earned inside your RRSP are taxed as regular income when withdrawn; these types of income lose their identity inside your RRSP; we call this investment amnesia.*
- *this does not mean you should avoid dividends and capital gains inside your RRSP since these will help to maximize your returns.*

How To Convert Taxable Income

So far we've talked a lot about the benefits of earning dividends and capital gains over interest income. But how do you practically make the move to income that's taxed at a lower rate? The next eight lessons should help.

LESSON 41

$▸$

Place maturing investments into equity mutual funds.

As your GICs, treasury bills, CSBs, and term deposits mature, consider investing some of the cash in equity mutual funds this time. Equities are investments that provide you with *ownership*. For example, buying common or preferred shares makes you an owner in the company. Investing in mutual funds that in turn buy common and preferred shares is also an equity investment. When you invest in equity mutual funds you avoid interest, open the door to dividends and capital gains, and receive the benefit of professional money management at the same time. We recommend that you buy one of the many guides to mutual funds that are typically published each fall for advice on specific funds, fund families, and how to buy them.

What We Have Learned:
- *as your interest-bearing investments mature, reinvest some of the money in equity mutual funds.*
- *equity mutual funds provide ownership in companies through investment in common and preferred shares.*
- *equity mutual funds avoid interest, open the door to dividends and capital gains, and offer professional money management.*

LESSON 42

$▸$

Re-invest in common or preferred shares.

An alternative to investing in mutual funds is to purchase individual stocks themselves. This will accomplish the same tax objective of converting interest to dividends. We should mention that there are a number of companies that offer decent rates of return on their dividends alone. For example, utilities companies usually offer high dividend yields. We recommend that you seek the advice of an experienced investment broker if you choose this route since very few of us have the time and expertise required to properly diversify and monitor our stock portfolios. Investing in stocks is something you should not consider unless you have in the neighbourhood of $15,000 to invest since it's difficult to diversify properly with less money. Mutual funds are ideal if you have less than $15,000.

What We Have Learned:
- *investing in individual stocks will achieve the tax objective of converting interest to dividends.*
- *seek the advice of an experienced investment broker when investing in individual stocks.*
- *stick to mutual funds unless you have $15,000 or more to invest.*

LESSON 43
Swap investments with your RRSP.

$▸$

If you have interest-bearing investments outside your RRSP that are not due to mature in the next couple of months, you should consider placing the investment inside your RRSP and taking out either cash, equity mutual funds, or stocks that you've been holding inside the plan. If you take out cash, you can immediately invest in equities that will provide you with dividends and potential capital gains. The advantage of this idea is that, where your money is locked into an interest-bearing investment for a length of time (as is the case with GICs), you can still manage to exchange it for equities that are taxed favourably. The swap with your RRSP will not result in any taxes owing because the contribution and withdrawal offset each other. One caution: by transferring investments to your RRSP you're actually making an RRSP contribution, so the value of the investment you're transferring to your RRSP must be within your available contribution room for the year (see lesson 53 for more details).

What We Have Learned:

- *where you have interest-bearing investments outside your RRSP that are not due to mature soon, contribute them to your RRSP and take out an equivalent amount of cash or equity investments to earn dividends and capital gains outside your RRSP.*
- *the swap can be done tax-free, but be sure you have adequate contribution room to do the swap.*

LESSON 44

Buy your home.

$▸$

Most Canadians have long believed that owning a home rather than renting makes sense. In almost every case this is true. Certainly there are tax advantages to owning rather than renting since investing in real estate will avoid interest income, and will provide the opportunity for capital gains (although some poor souls might argue with this!). What's more, the capital gains on your home will generally be tax-free if you designate the home as your *principal residence*. Tax-free capital gains are even better than dividends. Where you own more than one property, the principal residence rules become quite complex and you should visit a tax professional when selling a property to ensure that you haven't got a taxable capital gain.

The alternative is to rent your home, which will generally cost you a little less each month in cash payments. With the cash you save each month by renting you could invest in shares or equity mutual funds to provide a decent after-tax return. The only problem with the renting alternative is that, by investing the difference, you could never hope to match the after-tax return available from the tax-free capital gains offered when you own. At the end of the day, you're almost assured of having more to your name when you own than when you rent.

What We Have Learned:

- *investing in your home avoids interest income and provides capital gains that are, in most cases, tax-free.*
- *this conversion to tax-free capital gains is even better than the tax-favoured status of dividends.*

LESSON 45

Convert a loan or convertible debentures to share capital.

$⟩$

Perhaps you've made a loan to a corporation. If so, consider converting the loan to share capital where this option is available. Doing so will allow you to receive dividends rather than interest. Where you're already a shareholder the advantage may not be the same since you're already entitled to dividends, and chances are that the loan is interest-free so that you're not reporting interest income annually. If you're not currently a shareholder, approach the owner with the idea of converting your debt to *preferred shares*. To the owner of the company, your owning preferred shares with certain characteristics can be substantially the same as a loan from you.

Harvey Prefers Preferreds
Harvey loaned $5,000 to his brother's company. The company pays him 7% interest per year on the loan. Harvey decided to approach his brother with the idea of exchanging the loan for preferred shares in the company. Harvey's brother was hesitant because he didn't want to give up any ownership in the company. His concerns were laid to rest when the arrangement was structured so that Harvey had essentially the same rights, no more and no less, as he had with the loan. The preferred shares issued were 7% cumulative shares (to provide Harvey with the same annual income), non-voting (so Harvey had no control over the company), non-participating (so Harvey's shares did not increase in value as the company grew), and redeemable (so that his brother could pay Harvey off at any time and cancel the preferred shares). Harvey's brother did not give up any control, and Harvey received tax-favourable dividends instead of interest.

The exchange of a loan for shares *may* result in a disposition of the loan for tax purposes. Provided that the shares taken back are not worth more than the balance of the outstanding loan, there will not be any tax consequences on the exchange. Be sure to visit a tax professional if you decide to implement this idea.

Where you own a bond or debenture that has attached to it the right to convert into shares of the company (i.e. a convertible bond or debenture), you may want to consider making the conversion to reduce your tax exposure. Before doing this, be sure to decide whether the shares are a good investment themselves. A good investment broker should be able to help with this decision. Making the conversion will provide you with dividends rather than interest income.

What We Have Learned:
- *where you have made a loan to a corporation, approach the owner with the idea of converting to preferred shares so that you earn dividends rather than interest.*
- *this can be done in a manner that should be acceptable to the owner.*
- *where you own convertible bonds or debentures consider converting them to shares; assess the quality of the shares first.*

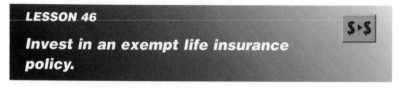

LESSON 46

Invest in an exempt life insurance policy.

We talked briefly about exempt life insurance policies in lesson 33, point 11. To recap, these policies offer the best of two worlds: insurance plus investments. The investment portion grows tax-free until you partially or fully dispose of the policy or borrow from it. If you hold the policy until you die, your beneficiaries receive all benefits tax-free. Any income earned inside the policy on the accumulated investments, whether it's interest, dividends, or capital gains, will be paid out tax-free when the policy matures on your death. In this case, you've converted investment income to tax-free income. Your beneficiaries will be the ones to enjoy the money. We'll talk more about exempt policies in lesson 125.

What We Have Learned:
- *exempt life insurance policies offer an investment component that grows tax-free.*
- *any investment income earned in the policy will be converted to a tax-free distribution to your beneficiaries on your death.*
- *your beneficiaries are the ones who will enjoy the money.*

LESSON 47

Convert the taxable portion of your annuity into a tax-free receipt.

$·$

If you receive periodic payments from an annuity, there are two things you should be looking for. We've come across both situations.

Situation 1

Take a good look at the T3 slip you've been receiving each year with respect to your annuity. Make sure that the taxable amount being included on the slip, and consequently on your tax return, is not the full amount of the payments you've been receiving. A portion of every annuity payment you receive is actually a return of your original capital, and so that portion is not taxable. We've seen situations where the issuing life insurance company has made a mistake on the T3 slip and designated the full amount of the payments as taxable. If you catch such a mistake, you can amend your tax returns for the last three years to correct the mistake. Further, although Revenue Canada does not normally permit you to go back more than three years to make changes, they might make an exception here to be fair to you – it's worth a try.

Situation 2

Remember that every annuity payment is split into two parts: a tax-free return of capital and an interest income portion. Only the interest is taxable. A few years ago we had a client who was receiving periodic annuity payments from an annuity that she had inherited. She was quite elderly, and her health took a turn for the worse. It was quite evident that there was no way she'd ever be able to recover all of her capital the annuity was expected to pay to her. As a result, we contacted Revenue Canada and argued that no portion of her annuity payments should be taxable. We argued that every cent of every payment she received was actually a return of her capital, and not interest. Revenue Canada bought the argument, and our client was able to convert taxable interest into a tax-free return of capital. We were able to amend her previous three years' tax returns and save her a significant amount of tax.

What We Have Learned:

- where you receive periodic payments from an annuity, be sure to check that only the interest portion of the payments is reflected as taxable on your T3 slip.
- where there's no possible way for you to recover the capital portion of your annuity, you might make the argument with Revenue Canada that no portion of your annuity payments should be subject to tax; this could effectively convert taxable interest into a tax-free return of capital.

LESSON 48

$▸$

When selling capital property, build interest into the sale price.

This idea goes hand in hand with an idea we introduced in lesson 34, point 15, so you'll want to refer there to fully understand this idea. It works this way: when you sell capital property you can defer taxes on any gain by taking payment over time in instalments. Since you're taking the payments in instalments, you might want to charge interest on the outstanding amounts periodically – this makes the idea of instalments more attractive. If you build the interest into the purchase price up front, you'll be taxed on the income as a capital gain, and not as interest – so you've successfully converted interest into a capital gain.

Matthew's Sale

Matthew found a buyer for his mint-condition 1957 Corvette that was once owned by his father, the original owner (we don't know why he'd sell such a car, but he did). Matthew agreed on a selling price of $20,000 and he arranged to take payment for the car over five years ($4,000 each year). Matthew wanted to earn 10% on the unpaid balance each year, and calculated (using a home computer program) that if he received $5,275 each year for five years, he'd earn that 10%. The buyer agreed, and Matthew set the selling price at $26,375 instead, to be paid over 5 years ($5,275 each year). The difference between the $26,375 final price and the $20,000 initially agreed price represents Matthew's interest for taking payment in instalments. Since Matthew's cost of the car is $10,000, he now has a $16,375 capital gain ($26,375-$10,000) that he'll pay tax on *over a five year period. He'll end up with more money in his pocket now than if he had reported the $6,375 ($26,375-$20,000) as interest income. He has converted interest into a capital gain.*

What We Have Learned:

- **when you sell capital property and take payment in instalments, build interest on the instalments into the selling price of the property to convert interest into capital gains.**
- **read lesson 34, point 15 to more fully understand this lesson.**

Part II

Special
Areas

Getting The Most From Your RRSP

7

An Introduction To RRSPs

From our experience, many people have misunderstandings about what a Registered Retirement Savings Plan (RRSP) is, how it should be used, and what to do with funds inside their RRSPs. In addition to answering these questions, we'll take a look at a number of more advanced issues related to your RRSP in this chapter.

LESSON 49

An RRSP is a vehicle only, not a specific investment.

An RRSP is a plan, registered with the government, to encourage and assist Canadians in saving for retirement. Many people confuse an RRSP as being a specific investment when it's actually a vehicle that is used to hold a variety of investments. There's no limit to the number of RRSPs you can open – you could have a separate RRSP for each investment if you wanted. The best way to understand the vehicle concept is to picture a basket. The basket is your RRSP. Now suppose you have $1,000 that you'd like to invest. You have a multitude of investments to choose from: GICs, treasury bills, term deposits, stocks, bonds, and mutual funds among other things. When you purchase the investment of your choice, you can hold it outside the basket, or you can hold it inside your RRSP basket. Every time you save or invest money, you have two decisions to make: (1) what type of investments should I hold? and (2) should I hold them inside or outside my RRSP?

What We Have Learned:
- *an RRSP is not a specific investment, it's a vehicle, or basket, used to hold investments of your choice.*
- *there is no limit to the number of RRSP baskets you can have.*
- *every time you save or invest, you must decide two things: what investments should I hold? And, should I hold them inside or outside my RRSP?*

LESSON 50

There are three important advantages to holding investments inside an RRSP.

Financial advisors are continually encouraging Canadians to contribute to their RRSPs. Despite this, the most recent statistics available from Revenue Canada tell us that just 24.9% of taxpayers are making RRSP contributions annually. This means that over three quarters of Canadian taxpayers are not currently contributing to an RRSP. With so many people opting against RRSPs, why are we recommending them? Because there are three very important advantages to putting money in your RRSP basket and then making investments there.

Current Tax Savings
When you make a contribution to your RRSP you're entitled to a deduction on your tax return for the amount of your contribution, provided it does not exceed certain limits. Because you're allowed a deduction for the amounts you contribute, you're not paying tax on these funds, and won't pay tax on the funds until the money is withdrawn from your RRSP. In effect, your deferral equals the tax you would've paid on those funds had you not made the contribution.

The amount of tax deferred can be easily calculated as the amount of your contribution multiplied by your marginal tax rate.

Tax-Free Accumulation
Once you've contributed to your RRSP, there will be no tax on the investment income that you earn inside the plan. The money is allowed to grow with taxes deferred until you make withdrawals from the plan. This tax-deferred compounding can make a big difference in the amount of money available to you when you retire. For example, if you invest $3,000 each year outside your RRSP, and earn 10% on your money, you'd have $199,307 after 30 years, assuming your marginal tax rate is 50%. Now invest the $3,000 in the same investments for the same length of time, but hold the investments inside your RRSP. After 30 years you'd have $493,482, almost two and a half times more than investing outside your RRSP. The advantage is too great to ignore.

Maintained Standard of Living
Provided you plan your RRSP contributions properly, you'll be able to maintain your standard of living when you retire. This is more than can be said for those who wait until the midnight hour to start saving, or for those who believe the government will be able to provide adequate income for daily living once you retire.

The truth is, you need to start early to accumulate enough capital to provide a decent retirement, and the task will be much easier with an RRSP than without one. Your tax professional or financial planner can help calculate what you'll need and how much to set aside each year to get you there.

As for government assistance – don't plan on getting much when you retire. Chances are, anything you get from the government will be so small, or start at such a late age, that it's better to plan as though you were not getting anything at all. Realize that 1995 represented the first year the Canada Pension Plan (CPP) paid out more in benefits than it brought in from taxpayers. The chief actuary of the Federal Office of the Superintendent of Financial Institutions has said that CPP premiums deducted from your pay and provided by your employer will have to increase from the current 5.6% of pensionable earnings to 11.8% in 2016, and 13.9% in 2030 to keep the plan afloat. In addition, we're told it may be necessary to push back the retirement age to 70 years old to help the problem.

Demographics don't bring good news either: there are fewer 18 year olds in Canada in 1996 than any other age group, and it's these youngsters who will be funding the government assistance so many of us expect. The rule to remember here: don't count on the government for retirement income unless you're retiring in the very near future.

What We Have Learned:
- *there are three important advantages to contributing to an RRSP: you experience immediate tax savings, tax-free accumulation of income, and you can maintain your standard of living at retirement with the help of such a plan.*
- *don't expect government assistance when planning for retirement.*

LESSON 51
RRSPs won't usually keep creditors away from your nestegg.

Before declaring bankruptcy, consider the effect it could have on your retirement savings. Any funds invested inside your RRSP are fair game when it comes to settling your debts (except in Prince Edward Island). This fact has clearly been established in the courts in recent years. There are some exceptions. Some RRSPs offered through insurance companies can offer creditor protection, although this may change in certain situations based on recent case law. Other exceptions are life and term annuities. Life annuities cannot be touched by creditors, and term annuities can pose a problem to them. Finally, funds in a Registered Retirement Income Fund (RRIF) can also offer protection from creditors.

If your financial situation is shaky and, as a result, you plan on converting your RRSP to an insurance-type plan, or to an annuity or RRIF to protect yourself immediately prior to declaring bankruptcy, you won't get the protection you're looking for. The law is designed to prevent this type of abuse – you'll need to make the conversion several years before declaring bankruptcy.

What We Have Learned:
- *creditors may be able to access assets in your RRSP if you declare bankruptcy.*
- *your insurance-type RRSP, annuity, or RRIF can offer protection from creditors.*
- *don't expect protection where you convert your RRSP to one of the aforementioned plans immediately prior to declaring bankruptcy.*

LESSON 52

RRSP administration fees should be paid outside your plan.

↓ $

Your RRSP must be administered by a trust company. This simply means that your bank, broker, or other institution negotiates with a trust company to hold your investments for you, in trust, until you retire or withdraw them. You'll pay an annual fee (for each RRSP) for this service, which most institutions fold into their GIC rates – that is, you'll get a slightly lower interest rate on your GICs to cover this administration charge. In the case of mutual funds, the annual fee is usually between $35 and $65 per year. Where your plan is a self-directed RRSP, the fee could range from $100 to $150 yearly.

Administration fees will be tax-deductible if they are paid outside of your RRSP. The other alternative is for the financial institution to take the fee out of the funds inside your RRSP – in fact, most mutual funds and brokers are set up to do this automatically. There are two problems with this: (1) it affects the growth of your investments inside the plan, and (2) the fee is not deductible for tax purposes. So, the rule is: take the initiative to ensure you're paying your fees with funds outside your RRSP.

What We Have Learned:
- *all RRSPs are administered by a trust company which charges a fee for this service each year.*
- *the fee varies, depending on the plan.*
- *always initiate the action necessary to pay this fee with funds outside your RRSP to ensure the fee is deductible.*

Contributing To Your RRSP

LESSON 53

Know your contribution limit each year.

The amount that you're eligible to contribute to your RRSP and deduct each year will depend on your *earned income*. Generally, you can contribute up to 18% of your prior years' earned income, or the yearly maximum, whichever is less. Once your earned income reaches a certain level, you'll be restricted to the maximum.

For example, if your earned income in 1995 was $75,000 or more, your RRSP contribution for 1996 will be limited to $13,500. Your Notice of Assessment received from Revenue Canada each year will detail the maximum you can contribute to your RRSP for the next year, so hold onto the assessment. The information on the assessment is generally reliable, but check it with your information, and if you have any questions see a tax professional. Maximum RRSP contributions for 1994 through 2000 along with the level of income at which the maximum limit kicks in are as follows (as an aside, keep your eye on the maximum contribution limits because they could change with future federal budgets).

Year	RRSP Contribution Limit	Earned Income needed for maximum contribution in following year
1994	$ 13,500	$ 80,555
1995	$ 14,500	$ 75,000
1996	$ 13,500	$ 75,000
1997	$ 13,500	$ 80,555
1998	$ 14,500	$ 86,111
1999	$ 15,500	indexed
2000	indexed	indexed

Earned Income

Your contribution is based on your *earned income* for the prior year. Calculating your earned income can be long and complex, but for the most part it will include employment income, self-employment income (subtract losses), royalties, research grants, net rental income (subtract losses), and alimony or separation payments received (subtract payments made). Earned income does *not* include investment income, taxable capital gains, pension or DPSP income, RRSP or RRIF income, OAS or CPP income (except disability CPP which qualifies), retiring allowances, death benefits, scholarships or bursaries, or income from a limited partnership. This information will be especially useful where you're in a position to control the types of income you receive – see lesson 54 for more details.

Your Pension Adjustment

Your RRSP contribution limit each year will be reduced where you participate in a pension plan or deferred profit sharing plan at work. Your employer is required to make a complicated calculation called your *pension adjustment* if you participate in one of these plans. This amount appears on your T4 slip each year. Your pension adjustment will reduce dollar for dollar your RRSP contribution limit. The idea behind this adjustment is that you'd otherwise have an unfair advantage over those without a pension plan if you could contribute to your plan at work and contribute the maximum limit each year to an RRSP at the same time. The pension adjustment puts all of us on a level playing field when saving for retirement. In the past, those with high incomes who participate in a pension plan at work have been able to contribute at least a token $1,000 to an RRSP. For 1996 and 1997 this $1,000 may not be available to you due to changes made to tax legislation in the February 1995 federal budget that reduced RRSP contribution levels for these years.

What We Have Learned:

- *your contribution limit each year is restricted to 18% of your earned income from the prior year, or the yearly maximum limit, whichever is less.*
- *your earned income can be a complex calculation.*
- *where you're involved in a pension plan or deferred profit sharing plan at work, your pension adjustment will reduce your RRSP contribution limit.*

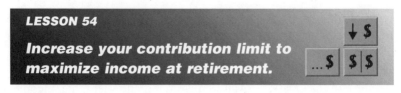

LESSON 54

Increase your contribution limit to maximize income at retirement.

If you are your own boss, operate through a corporation, and want to increase your RRSP contributions, try paying yourself a bonus or increasing your salary. This will increase your earned income and provide you with more contribution room. More contribution room allows for greater contributions to your RRSP and more income at retirement.

Don't forget that once your income reaches a certain level, your contributions are limited to the yearly maximum. Refer again to the table on page 98 for those income levels. It wouldn't make sense, for example, to increase your salary to provide RRSP contribution room if your salary is already $75,000 or more in 1996 since you've already reached the 1997 maximum contribution limit of $13,500. You can also increase your earned income by reducing the rental losses or self-employment losses you claim. These losses can be reduced by, for example, paying down your home mortgage (to reduce the interest deduction you claim each year), or by reducing voluntary deductions.

What We Have Learned:
- *increasing your earned income will provide more RRSP contribution room and allow for more savings at retirement.*
- *increase your earned income when you're self-employed by paying yourself a bonus or increasing your salary.*
- *increase earned income by reducing rental losses or self-employment losses.*

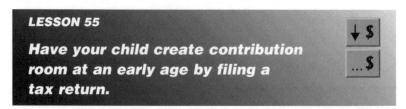

LESSON 55

Have your child create contribution room at an early age by filing a tax return.

Generally, there's no requirement to file a tax return unless you owe taxes. In the past, many children who have earned wages by working part-time have not bothered to file tax returns since there was no point in going through the paperwork when no taxes were owing. We recommend that your child file a tax return, even when no taxes are owing and no refund is due, strictly to create contribution room for his or her RRSP. Is it really worth it?

Bobby's Summer Job

Last summer, at the age of 15, Bobby started his own lawn-cutting business. In the summer months he made about $1,200. Although Bobby didn't earn enough to be taxable, he filed a tax return anyway. Filing a tax return resulted in RRSP contribution room of $216 (18% of $1,200) last year. By the time Bobby was 19, he had accumulated $1,600 of RRSP contribution room. When he graduated from university at age 22 and began working full time, he made a contribution of $1,600 to an RRSP and increased his refund that year by $432. His friends, who graduated at the same time, were not eligible to contribute to an RRSP in their first year out of school since they had no contribution room. Bobby also had a head start saving for retirement, and the $1,600 contribution will amount to $170,750 if he allows it to compound at 10% per year until he's 71 years of age.

What We Have Learned:
• **filing a tax return each year that your child has earned income will create valuable contribution room that will save taxes later.**

LESSON 56

Start your RRSP contributions as early in life as possible.

Curiosity may have killed the cat, but it's procrastination that will hurt the retiree. Time can be your biggest ally in saving for retirement. Start when you're young and you can significantly reduce the portion of your income that you need to set aside to retire. It's much easier to set aside $2,000 a year from the time you start working full time than setting aside $15,000 a year from the age of 50 to 65. By the way, you'd end up with much more money at retirement in the first case than the second.

Peter's Procrastination

Margie and Peter were both 30 years old. Margie decided it was time to put some money aside for retirement, so from the age of 30 to 36 (a total of seven years), Margie set aside $1,000 each year ($7,000 in total). From the age of 36 to 65 Margie's $7,000 grew to $165,542 inside her RRSP. Peter waited until age 36 to think about retirement, at which time he set aside $1,000 each year from age 36 to 65, a total of 30 years and $30,000 in contributions. When Peter retired at age 65, he had $164,494. Margie actually ended up with $1,048 more than Peter even though she had only contributed $7,000 compared to his $30,000. They both earned the same rate of return on their investments – 10% per year. If Peter had contributed the same $30,000 but had started 6 years earlier when Margie had started, he would've had $126,917 more at retirement than what he ended up with.

If you haven't yet begun setting aside money in your RRSP, don't panic. You can still accumulate a decent nestegg if you have a few years left before you retire, but start today because five years of tax-free compounding makes a big difference. In fact, five years is enough time to double your nestegg if you earn an average of 14.9% per year on your money over that period.

What We Have Learned:
- *start contributing to your RRSP as soon as possible.*
- *procrastination can significantly reduce money available at retirement.*
- *if you haven't yet started saving for retirement, don't panic, but open an RRSP today because five years can make a world of difference at retirement.*

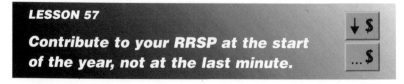

LESSON 57

Contribute to your RRSP at the start of the year, not at the last minute.

You're able to make contributions to your RRSP in the year and within 60 days following the year. So, if you want to make a contribution and claim a deduction for it on your 1996 tax return, your contribution will have to be made in 1996 or up until March 1, 1997, but no later.

By waiting until the last minute you actually cheat yourself out of tax-free earnings. Suppose you want to contribute $3,600 to your RRSP for 1996 and you do this by contributing at the start of 1996 rather than waiting until March 1, 1997 to make the contribution. Over the course of 1996 you could earn about $360 in income on your contribution at a 10% rate of return. Why give up $360 when all you have to do is contribute at the start of the year? If you haven't got the money up front, you should consider contributing monthly instead of making a last-minute lump-sum payment. In our example, you could make contributions of $300 each month instead of $3,600 on March 1, 1997. Doing this could provide about $170 in tax-free income that you would not have received by making a last minute contribution. Not as good as making the payment at the start of the year, but much better than making a last-minute effort.

Rob Contributes Early

Rob is 30 years old and plans on retiring at age 65. He decided to contribute $3,600 to his RRSP for 1996. Rather than waiting until March 1, 1997, he made the contribution in January 1996. Rob has decided to continue this practice of contributing $3,600 early in each year, until he retires. When he retires at age 65, Rob will have $1,073,256 assuming a rate of return of 10% per year. If Rob were to wait until the last minute each year to contribute his $3,600, he would have $975,688 at retirement. He can increase his savings at retirement by a full $97,568 if he contributes at the start of each year. If instead he makes equal monthly payments of $300 ($3,600 per year) until age 65, he would have $1,027,768 – better than contributing at the last minute, but still $45,488 less than contributing at the start of each year.

What We Have Learned:
- **deductible contributions to your RRSP must be made in the year or within 60 days after the year end.**
- **you could end up with significantly more money at retirement by contributing at the start of each year than by waiting until the last minute to contribute.**
- **even contributing monthly throughout the year is better than contributing at the last minute.**

LESSON 58

Use up unused contribution room before it's gone forever.

Each year that you have earned income you create contribution room for yourself. Contribution room is simply the amount that you're able to contribute to your RRSP without paying a penalty. You can use up your contribution room simply by making a contribution to your RRSP. If you don't make a contribution to your plan, your contribution room can be carried forward for up to seven years, perhaps to a year when you have more cash available to make contributions. Beyond seven years, your contribution room will begin to expire – it will be lost forever.

It seems that most people who allow their contribution room to carry forward never actually use up the room, and consequently give up the deduction that the contribution room provides. We recommend that you use up your contribution room as it's created, to avoid losing it altogether. This may mean borrowing to contribute if necessary.

What We Have Learned:
- *each year that you have earned income you create RRSP contribution room for yourself.*
- *unused contribution room can be carried forward up to seven years at which time it will expire.*
- *most people who carry forward contribution room never use it up and lose the deduction available to them.*
- *try to use up your contribution room as it's created, even if you have to borrow to do this.*

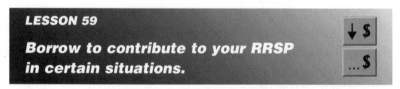

LESSON 59

Borrow to contribute to your RRSP in certain situations.

We're often asked whether it makes sense to borrow to contribute to an RRSP. Generally, you'll be better off borrowing to make a contribution than not making a contribution at all. As mentioned earlier, your available contribution room will expire after seven years if not used, and in this case it's certainly better to borrow to use up the room than to let it expire. In addition, you'll be better off to borrow for your contributions than to wait a few years before using up your contribution room since you'll benefit from tax-fee compounding that much sooner.

If you do borrow to contribute, keep in mind two important points: (1) the interest on the loan is not deductible for tax purposes, and (2) it's important to pay the loan back within one year. Since the interest on RRSP loans is not deductible, you'll be better off borrowing for the investments you hold *outside* your RRSP where you're permitted an interest deduction. Extending the loan beyond one year means more interest costs to you and will further limit the benefit of borrowing to contribute. In addition, if you're borrowing every year to contribute, and each loan extends beyond one year, your debt load could quickly multiply. Use your tax refund to pay down the RRSP loan to reduce the payback period.

One last comment. If you're going to borrow for RRSP contributions, you'll probably be making monthly payments to your bank to pay back the loan. If your cash flow will allow you to handle a monthly payment of, say, $250, then try contributing the $250 directly to your RRSP each month instead, and pay down the bank loan with a salary increase or bonus you might have received – generally you'll be just as well off making these monthly payments to your RRSP as you would've been had you borrowed to contribute a larger amount up-front. Why? Because you'll save interest costs, and for many people, less debt means better sleep at night.

What We Have Learned:

- *borrowing to contribute to your RRSP makes sense where you would not otherwise contribute, where your contribution room is about to expire, or where you'd otherwise wait several years before using up your contribution room.*
- *interest on such loans is not deductible, so consider borrowing for the investments you hold outside your RRSP instead.*
- *pay back all RRSP loans within one year; use your refund to pay down the loan.*
- *consider making monthly contributions to your RRSP rather than using the cash to make monthly payments on a loan from the bank.*

LESSON 60
Over-contribute to your RRSP by $2,000.   ...$

While contributing too much to your RRSP can result in penalties of
1% per month of the excess amount, the government does provide
a cushion of $2,000. This means that you can actually over-con-
tribute to your RRSP by $2,000 without a problem. The cushion
used to be $8,000, but the limit was changed in the February 1995
federal budget and became effective January 1, 1996. Where you're
in a position to maximize your contributions each year, you can certainly benefit by over-contributing. You won't be allowed a deduction for the over-contribution, but the $2,000 will grow tax-free
inside your RRSP and will more than make up for the lack of deduction as long as you have at least five years to go before retirement. In
fact, a $2,000 over-contribution could increase your retirement sav-
ings by $34,899 at 10% per year, if you have 30 years to go before
retirement. Many taxpayers took advantage of this idea when the
cushion was $8,000, so if you've over-contributed in the past, be
sure to visit your tax professional right away to find out whether or
not you're in excess of the new, lower $2,000 limit.

What We Have Learned:
• *the government allows over-contributions of up to $2,000 to your
RRSP without penalties.*
• *where you're in a position to maximize your RRSP contributions
each year and you have at least five years to go before retirement, an over-contribution will provide you with additional
income at retirement.*

LESSON 61
Contribute every year, but consider delaying the deduction.   ↓$ ...$

Let's clear up some confusion about RRSPs. Try to separate in your
mind RRSP contributions from the corresponding deduction. You
can make contributions as long as you have contribution room available, but you don't have to take a deduction for the contribution

until you want to – there are no time restrictions at all. This means that, where you expect your marginal tax rate to rise significantly in the next year or two, it may be worth putting off the deduction until that year.

Greer Called to the Bar

Greer made an RRSP contribution of $5,000 this year. Her marginal tax rate is 27%, so claiming a deduction for the contribution this year will save her $1,350 in taxes ($5,000 x 27%). Greer expects her income to grow significantly two years from now after she passes her bar exams and begins working full time for a high profile law firm downtown. She expects her marginal tax rate to climb to 45% at that time. Instead of taking the deduction for her RRSP contribution this year, she has decided to wait for two years. When she takes the deduction two years from now, her tax savings will be $2,250 ($5,000 x 45%). Her tax savings are increased by $900 by waiting two years. The cost to her is about $140 – the after-tax income she could have earned on the $1,350 tax savings had she taken the deduction this year. The net benefit to Greer is cash in her pocket of $760 ($900 – $140).

Delaying your RRSP deduction will also make sense when you expect the government to increase tax rates in the next year or two since, as in Greer's example above, the higher tax rate will give rise to larger tax savings from the deduction.

What We Have Learned:
- *you don't need to take a deduction for RRSP contributions in the year you make the contribution.*
- *consider delaying the deduction where you expect that, in the next couple of years, your marginal tax rate will rise or the government will increase tax rates, since your tax savings will be increased.*

LESSON 62

Contribute to your RRSP and use the refund to pay down your mortgage.

The question of whether to pay down your mortgage or contribute to your RRSP is pondered even more often than *which came first, the chicken or the egg?* The good news is that we can actually calculate an answer to the first question. The answer depends on many factors, and will differ for every person, but the first place to start is by asking yourself the question: *will I use my tax savings to pay down my mortgage?*

Applying Your Tax Savings to Your Mortgage

When you contribute to your RRSP you're entitled to a deduction on your tax return. This deduction will create tax savings that, more often than not, come back to you as a refund in April when you file your tax return (your tax savings will equal your contribution amount multiplied by your marginal tax rate). Where you apply the tax savings to pay down your mortgage you're really getting the best of both worlds – an RRSP contribution *plus* a reduction in your mortgage. It's clear to us that when you contribute to your RRSP *and* use your refund to pay down your mortgage you will, in virtually every case, be better off than paying down your mortgage alone.

Using Your Tax Savings for Other Things

If you choose not to apply your tax savings to pay down your mortgage, you'll still be better off in most cases contributing to your RRSP *unless* two conditions are met:
1. your mortgage rate is 3% or more above the rate of return inside your RRSP, *and*
2. you'll invest two thirds or more of all your annual mortgage payments in an RRSP once your mortgage is paid off.

Aside from the math, there may be good reasons to contribute to your RRSP rather than paying down your mortgage. These include: improved diversification (not all your money is in real estate), better liquidity (RRSP investments can be converted to cash more quickly than your home), RRSPs are a source of short-term cash flow (due to the refund often resulting from a contribution), and RRSPs can provide income during no or low income stages in life.

What We Have Learned:
• *it's better to contribute to your RRSP and use the tax savings to pay down your mortgage than to pay down your mortgage alone.*
• *if you don't use your tax savings to pay down your mortgage, it's still better to contribute to your RRSP, unless your mortgage rate is 3% or more above your RRSP's rate of return and you'll be*

investing at least two thirds of your mortgage payments inside your RRSP once the mortgage is paid off.

• *aside from the math, there are other good reasons to contribute to your RRSP rather than your mortgage.*

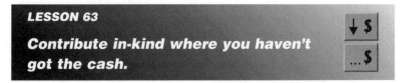

LESSON 63

Contribute in-kind where you haven't got the cash.

Many people don't realize that they are able to contribute more than just money to an RRSP. In fact, any qualified investment can be contributed and provide a deduction, just as though you had contributed cash. This makes good sense where you have investments outside your RRSP but don't have the cash to make a contribution. For tax purposes, transferring investments to your RRSP will result in a disposition of that investment, and could trigger a taxable capital gain where the investment has appreciated in value. You'll need to set up a self-directed RRSP in most cases where you want to contribute in-kind, but this can be done easily by visiting your local financial institution.

The list of investments that qualify to be contributed in-kind is long, and while the list below is not all-inclusive, it highlights some of the more common ones.

QUALIFIED RRSP INVESTMENTS

• cash
• shares listed on a prescribed Canadian stock exchange
• shares listed on a prescribed foreign stock exchange
• units of many mutual funds
• shares of Canadian public companies not listed on a prescribed stock exchange
• government or government guaranteed debt obligations
• corporate bonds or other debt obligations
• GICs
• a mortgage secured by real property in Canada, including your own home mortgage if insured

• certain annuities
• certain life insurance policies
• certain rights or warrants
• shares of certain small business corporations (some restrictions apply)

We recommend that you speak to your tax professional before contributing any investment in-kind to be sure of the tax consequences and since holding non-qualified investments inside your RRSP can result in income being taxed inside the RRSP, the value of the investment being taxed in your hands, or deregistration of the plan.

What We Have Learned:
• *contributions to your RRSP don't have to be in cash.*
• *any qualified investment can be contributed in-kind to your RRSP and provide a deduction.*
• *contributing in-kind may give rise to taxable capital gains where the property being contributed has appreciated in value.*
• *contributing in-kind makes sense where you have investments outside your RRSP and no cash to make a contribution.*

Special Contributions And Rollovers

LESSON 64

Rollover a retiring or termination allowance into your RRSP.

When you receive a retiring or termination allowance, a portion of the payment can be contributed to your RRSP. Rolling such a payment into your RRSP can be done, up to certain limits, on top of your usual RRSP contribution limit. The amount you're able to transfer is $2,000 for each year (or partial year) of your employment up to 1995, plus an additional $1,500 for each year (or partial year) before 1989 that you were employed by the same employer and for which your employer's contributions to an RPP or DPSP had not vested.

Your employer is required to provide a T4A slip (not a T4) for the allowance, and is supposed to calculate any portion *not* eligible for a rollover to your RRSP and note this amount on the slip. Employers often make errors when calculating the ineligible amount reported on the T4A slip, so check it for reasonableness and question the amount if it appears wrong. If a mistake has been made, your employer will have to issue a new slip, otherwise you could face difficulties in dealing with Revenue Canada. The amount of the allowance is included in your income in the year you receive it, but an offsetting deduction can be claimed where you rolled it into your RRSP. The transfer to your RRSP does not have to be made directly – you can take the retiring or termination allowance into your hands and then contribute it to your RRSP, as long as this is done within 60 days after the end of the year in which you received the payment. See more details in lesson 33, point 6.

What We Have Learned:
* *retiring and termination allowances can be rolled into an RRSP, up to certain limits; the transfer does not have to be done directly.*
* *the contribution can be made over and above your regular contribution limit.*
* *be sure the allowance is correctly reported on a T4A slip, or you'll need a new one.*

LESSON 65

Roll funds from your RPP to your RRSP.   **... $**

There are generally four situations that can arise where you'll be able to transfer funds from a Registered Pension Plan (RPP) to an RRSP: (1) when you leave your employer, (2) upon marriage break-down, (3) upon death of the plan member, and (4) upon a return of pre-1991 contributions. In each case, it's very important that the funds be transferred directly to the RRSP, and not paid out to you and then contributed to the RRSP.

Leaving Your Employer
This is the most common situation that arises. Where you leave your employer for any reason, including retirement or "restructuring",

you'll be able to transfer a certain amount from your RPP to an RRSP. This amount is generally calculated as the present value of the lifetime benefits you're entitled to receive from your RPP. The funds will have to be transferred to a *locked-in* RRSP in most cases. *Locked-in* means just that – you won't be able to make ad-hoc withdrawals. The rationale is that the funds transferred to your RRSP should be subject the same rules that governed your RPP – so your options for accessing your money will generally be limited to a life annuity or a Life Income Fund (LIF) – see lesson 82 for more details on LIFs.

It's worth mentioning that there may be situations where transferring RPP funds to an RRSP is possible without leaving your employer, but generally this is discouraged under the rules governing most RPPs.

Marriage Break-Down
A lump-sum transfer from your RPP to your spouse's RRSP can be made on a tax-free basis when the transfer is done directly, and where it's done by way of a court order or a written separation agreement.

Death of Plan Member
Where the member of an RPP has died, a lump-sum transfer to the RRSP (or RPP for that matter) of the surviving spouse can be made on a tax-free basis as long as it's done directly.

Return of Pre-1991 Contributions
Where you made contributions to an RPP prior to 1991 you may be entitled to a tax-free rollover of those contributions (plus accumulated interest) to your RRSP. This law was introduced to accommodate those taxpayers who participate in RPPs that are amended to retroactively reduce or eliminate the requirement for plan members to make contributions.

Where you've got the option of either taking your RPP funds and rolling them into an RRSP or simply taking the annual benefits provided by your pension plan, you'll need to do some calculations to figure out which is better. If you're numerically challenged, you might want to visit a tax professional to have the calculation done for you.

If you can do the calculation yourself, you'll need to compare the present value of the lifetime pension benefits you'll receive if you stay in the RPP to the amount of the lump-sum you'd get if you chose the RRSP option. One benefit to the RRSP option is that you might be able to earn an excellent rate of return with the help of a good investment broker, which could provide you with more income than the RPP itself would provide, although this requires an actuarial calculation.

There's one other situation that could result in a tax-free rollover out of an RPP, although the rollover cannot be made to an RRSP. Where the member of an RPP dies and a lump-sum becomes payable out of the RPP to a child or grandchild under the age of 18, the payment can be used to buy an annuity providing payments to the child to age 18, but cannot be transferred to an RRSP for the child. The payment does not have to be made directly in this case, but can be paid to the child without tax consequences as long as the annuity is purchased within 60 days after the end of the year the payment was received. Where the same lump-sum has been left to an adult child or grandchild (over 18 years of age), there are no tax-free transfers available at all.

You should be aware that whenever you're entitled to a tax-free rollover from an RPP to an RRSP, you'll almost certainly be able to make the same transfer to another RPP instead, if this suits your situation better.

What We Have Learned:
- *there are generally four situations that will provide an opportunity for a tax-free rollover from your RPP to an RRSP: when you leave your employer, upon marriage break-down, upon death of the plan member, and where you have pre-1991 contributions.*
- *where you have a choice to stay in your RPP or roll the money into an RRSP, a complex calculation will need to be done to determine which is better.*
- *transfers to minor children can also be made tax-free, but not to an RRSP.*

LESSON 66

Roll receipts from a United States IRA into your RRSP.

An Individual Retirement Account (IRA) in the United States is the American equivalent to our Canadian RRSP. If you've been earning income in the United States and have contributed to an IRA, but are now a Canadian resident, you'll be taxed, in both countries, on any withdrawals from your IRA. The Canadian government introduced rules that became effective July 13, 1990 that will allow you to transfer funds from your IRA to another IRA, or to an RRSP without paying tax. The tax-free rollover to your RRSP can be made to the extent the payment is derived from a previous contribution to your IRA in the U.S. by you, your spouse, or a former spouse. You'll make your life more simple by rolling your IRA into an RRSP rather than keeping the IRA and having plans in both countries. You might need guidance in dealing with your U.S. financial institution since they may need an education on how the rules apply to Canadian residents.

What We Have Learned:
- *where you've contributed to a United States IRA you're able to make a tax-free rollover to your RRSP provided the payment is derived from a previous contribution to your IRA by you, your spouse, or former spouse.*
- *you'll make your life more simple by rolling your IRA into an RRSP rather than having plans in both countries.*

LESSON 67

Roll inherited RRSP funds into your own RRSP, RRIF, or annuity.

Where you inherit the RRSP funds of a family member, you may be able to roll the full amount into your own RRSP, RRIF, or annuity, saving the deceased from paying tax on the investment. Where you're the spouse of the deceased you'll have an easier time doing this than the children will. In fact, the children will, in most cases, only receive the RRSP funds after the taxman has taken his share.

Inherited by Spouse

If you're the surviving spouse, the full amount of your deceased spouse's RRSP (called a *refund of premiums*) can be transferred to your own RRSP if you're under 72 years of age, or to a RRIF, life annuity, or term annuity, where you're 72 years of age or better. Transfers to your plan must be made in the year the funds are received, or within 60 days after the year end. There will be no tax on the funds until they are withdrawn from your own RRSP, RRIF, or annuity. Leaving RRSP funds to a surviving spouse is the easiest way to avoid tax upon death. All you need to do is name your spouse as beneficiary under the plan or in your will, but the former is preferred.

Inherited by Children or Grandchildren

Where there's no surviving spouse, RRSP funds are most commonly left to children or grandchildren. In most cases, the funds will be taxed in the hands of the deceased on his or her last tax return, with the remaining funds going to the child. There's one exception to this rule. Where the child or grandchild (including an adult) was "financially dependent" on the deceased at the time of death, the full RRSP funds can be transferred to the child's own RRSP. If the child is a minor, the funds can only be used to provide an annuity to age 18, and not for contribution to an RRSP, unless the child was dependent due to a physical or mental infirmity. In the absence of such an infirmity, a child will be considered dependent where the child's income is less than $6,456, or where the facts of the situation support the claim of dependency. There is no definition of *dependency* in the tax law, so there's room for creativity here. Again, tax-free rollovers must be made in the year the funds are received or within 60 days after year end.

What We Have Learned:

- *RRSP funds inherited by a surviving spouse can be rolled into an RRSP, RRIF, or annuity for the survivor on a tax-free basis.*
- *RRSP funds inherited by a child or grandchild will be taxed in the deceased's hands first, then paid to the child, unless the child was "financially dependent" on the deceased at the time of death, in which case a tax-free rollover may take place.*

LESSON 68

Roll your RRSP funds into another RRSP, tax-free.

There are a number of reasons why you might decide to transfer your RRSP funds to a different RRSP. The most common situation is where you're unhappy with the performance of your investments, and you decide to put the money where it will earn a higher return. Another common situation arises when you've accumulated enough money in your RRSP to make it worth moving to a self-directed plan (we'll talk about these shortly). Regardless of your reason for switching from one RRSP to another, the transfer can be done without any tax consequences, but beware, you must be sure to have the transfer done directly rather than withdrawing your funds from your old RRSP and then contributing to the new plan.

Mike's Mistake

*Mike was not pleased with the performance of his RRSP investments over the past five years. Mike was so unhappy with their performance that he decided to withdraw the full $15,000 in his plan right away to avoid further declines in value. Mike then opened a new plan with a reputable investment broker and handed him the $15,000 to begin investing right away. Mike's mistake cost him $2,500 of his retirement savings. Did you catch it? Mike's $15,000 withdrawal from his old RRSP was taxable in the year he withdrew it. He thought he would be all right since he turned around and made a $15,000 contribution to a new RRSP which would provide an offsetting deduction. Bad move! Mike's contribution limit for the year was only $10,000, giving him a $10,000 deduction only. The other $5,000 was taxable income to him, and he paid $2,500 in taxes as a result since his marginal tax rate is 50%. In addition, Mike used up valuable contribution room that would not have been used had he done things properly. Mike could have avoided tax on the rollover to his new RRSP and preserved his contribution room by arranging for the funds to be transferred **directly** to his new RRSP. His investment broker could have arranged this for him.*

What We Have Learned:

• *there are a number of reasons why you might close one RRSP and open another.*

• *funds can be transferred from one RRSP to another on a tax-free basis, but should be done directly, rather than withdrawing from one plan and contributing to the new plan.*

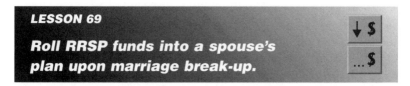

LESSON 69

Roll RRSP funds into a spouse's plan upon marriage break-up.

It's a common occurrence when a marriage breaks-up for one spouse to make an equalization payment to the other. If you and your spouse have separated, or are divorced, any investments in your RRSP can be transferred on a tax-free basis to your spouse's plan. Further, amounts in your RRSP can be rolled into RRIFs or a registered pension plan of your spouse without any tax consequences. Before you go ahead with any transfers, remember that the rollover must be direct from your RRSP to your spouse's, and the payment must be made pursuant to a decree, order or judgement of a competent tribunal, or a written separation agreement.

Normally, transferring funds to your spouse can become a problem under the *attribution rules* (see chapter 4), but these rules won't apply where the RRSP rollover takes place upon separation or divorce. In addition, the rules discouraging withdrawals from a spousal RRSP (we'll talk about these shortly) are avoided in this situation.

What We Have Learned:
• *direct transfers from your RRSP to your spouse's can be made on a tax-free basis upon marriage break-up.*
• *the payment must be pursuant to a decree, order or judgement of a competent tribunal, or a written separation agreement.*

Spousal RRSPs

LESSON 70

Your spouse's RRSP and a spousal RRSP are two different things.

Try not to get confused between your spouse's RRSP and a spousal RRSP. Your *spouse's RRSP* is a plan that he or she contributes to and that your spouse will receive payments from when he or she retires. Your spouse will be entitled to the deduction for any contributions, subject to his or her contribution limits. A *spousal RRSP*, on the other hand, is a plan that *you* contribute to under which your spouse is the annuitant (your spouse receives the income from the plan at his or her retirement). You're the one who gets the deduction since you make the contributions. Contributing to a spousal plan does not entitle you to more contribution room. That is, all contributions to a spousal plan combined with contributions to your own plan cannot exceed your contribution limit for the year. The real advantage of contributing to a spousal RRSP is that you're splitting income. The future retirement income is moved from your hands and taxed in your spouse's hands. There's also a deferral of taxable income because your spouse won't be taxed on the money until he or she takes it out of the plan at retirement.

What We Have Learned:
- *a spousal RRSP is a plan that you contribute to under which your spouse is the annuitant.*
- *you can claim a deduction for contributions to such a plan, but all contributions to the plan must be within your available contribution limit for the year.*
- *contributions to a spousal RRSP will reduce, split and defer taxable income.*

LESSON 71

The higher-income spouse should contribute to a spousal RRSP.

Deciding which spouse should make contributions to a spousal RRSP is easy. The higher-income spouse should make such contributions for three reasons. See if you can spot them.

Mark and Karen

Mark and Karen are married. Mark is the higher income earner and has more disposable income available than Karen, and so he decided to open *a spousal RRSP for her. In 1996 he contributed $5,000 to the plan. Mark's contribution provided him with tax savings of $2,500 in 1996 since his marginal tax rate is 50%. The income will grow tax-free until Karen withdraws the money later in life. At that time, the money will be taxed in her hands at her marginal tax rate, which is just 27%. The $5,000 will grow to be $140,512 in 35 years, at 10% per year, when Mark and Karen are 65 years old, so Karen will pay tax of $37,938 ($140,512 x 27%) when she withdraws the money over time. If Mark had to pay tax on this withdrawal, it would amount to $70,256 ($140,512 x 50%). The couple will save $32,318 in taxes by putting the withdrawal in Karen's hands rather than Mark's. Finally, Mark could have paid tax on the $5,000 the year he earned it, but managed to defer tax until they were 65 when Karen made the withdrawal.*

Did you spot the three reasons why the higher income earner should make a spousal RRSP contribution? First, it's the higher-income spouse that will usually have enough cash to make such a contribution. Second, the higher-income spouse will get a deduction while the annuitant spouse will get the eventual inclusion in income, presumably at a lower marginal tax rate, so there's a splitting of income. Finally, the income won't be taxed in the annuitant spouse's hands for a number of years, so there's a deferral.

What We Have Learned:
- **the higher-income spouse should contribute to a spousal RRSP for three good reasons: this spouse usually has more disposable income to make a contribution, you'll split income since the lower-income spouse will pay the tax later, and you'll defer income since your spouse won't be taxed until he or she retires.**

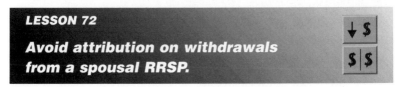

LESSON 72

Avoid attribution on withdrawals from a spousal RRSP.

Picture this. You contribute to a spousal RRSP in July 1996. Then your spouse withdraws the money from the plan one week later to spend on 15 pairs of new shoes. You get a deduction on your 1996 tax return for the contribution, and your spouse, who has no other income, reports the RRSP withdrawal as income, pays no tax, and has some great looking shoes. Great idea – you've effectively deducted the cost of your spouse's shoes on your tax return! The idea is too good in fact. For this reason, the Minister of Finance decided back in 1977 that this type of abuse would not be allowed.

The tax law says that if your spouse withdraws funds from a spousal plan that you contributed to, you (and not your spouse) will be taxed on the withdrawal (or a portion of it) if you had made any contributions to a spousal plan in the year of the withdrawal or the two immediately preceding years. The amount included in your income will be the lesser of (1) the amount withdrawn by your spouse, or (2) the total of all contributions made by you to a spousal plan in the year of withdrawal and the preceding two years. The excess, if any, will be taxed in your spouse's hands. As long as you have not made any contributions to a spousal plan in the year of withdrawal or the preceding two years, you won't have to worry about attribution back to you. So our July 1996 spousal RRSP contribution can be withdrawn without attribution if we wait until January 1, 1999.

What We Have Learned:
- *withdrawals from a spousal RRSP may be taxed in the contributor's hands if any contributions were made to a spousal plan in the year of withdrawal or the preceding two years.*

LESSON 73

Always contribute to a spousal RRSP by December 31st of each year.

There may be times when you'd like to take money out of a spousal RRSP. For example, when one spouse is at home looking after a newborn child the extra income could be useful. The problem is, you'll generally have to wait three years before withdrawing the funds to avoid the attribution problem we mentioned in the last lesson. You can effectively reduce this three year waiting period to two years by making contributions by December 31st each year.

Rob, Kathy, and Junior
Rob and Kathy are a young couple who'd like to have a child in the next couple of years. Rob has been contributing to a spousal RRSP for Kathy for the last three years. Rob's last contribution was on December 31, 1995. In the fall of 1997 their wish came true and they had a bouncing baby boy. Since Kathy decided to stay home with the baby, she would have no income in 1998. Since the couple needed extra income, Kathy withdrew $6,500 on January 1, 1998 from the spousal plan Rob had been contributing to. The $6,500 will be taxed in Kathy's hands (not Rob's) since Rob had not made a contribution to the plan in the year of the withdrawal (1998) or the preceding two years (1996 or 1997). The best part is, the $6,500 was only tied up in the plan for two years, plus a day (December 31, 1995 to January 1, 1998). If Rob had made his last contribution to the spousal RRSP one day later, on January 1, 1996, Kathy could not have made a withdrawal and avoided attribution until 1999, a full year later. By the way, the $6,500 is income to Kathy in 1998, but won't result in any tax due the basic personal credit of $6,456 available to all Canadians.

What We Have Learned:
• **there are times when you may want to access the funds inside a spousal RRSP.**
• **contributing by December 31st of each year will enable you to effectively reduce the waiting period from three years to two years before you can make the withdrawal without attribution.**

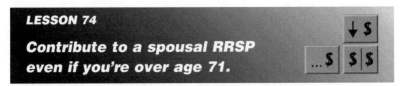

LESSON 74

***Contribute to a spousal RRSP
even if you're over age 71.***

An RRSP is a vehicle that's good until the year you turn age 71. In that year, you're able to make one last RRSP contribution, but by December 31st of the same year you'll have to collapse your plan. There are a few options available to avoid being taxed all at once on the funds in your RRSP the year you turn 71, and we'll be looking at this in lesson 82. If you've reached age 71 and still have contribution room that hasn't been used up, you can still make a contribution to a spousal RRSP, and take a deduction for it, up to and including the year your spouse turns age 71. The benefit of making this kind of contribution, of course, is that the deduction is available beyond age 71 where normally a contribution to your own RRSP cannot be made.

What We Have Learned:

- *contributions to your own RRSP can be made up to and including the year you turn age 71, but your plan must be collapsed by December 31st of that year and no contributions or related deductions can be made after that year.*
- *you can still claim a deduction for RRSP contributions after age 71 if you contribute to a spousal RRSP up to and including the year your spouse turns age 71.*

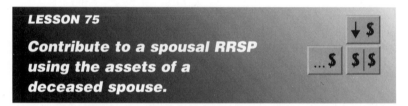

LESSON 75

Contribute to a spousal RRSP using the assets of a deceased spouse.

You'd think that once a person has died, he can no longer contribute to an RRSP. Not quite true. Revenue Canada holds the view that where an individual has died, the executor or legal representative of the estate can make a contribution to a spousal RRSP using the deceased's assets. Of course, the contribution must be made in the year the surviving spouse turns age 71 or before. Further, any contributions must be made within the usual contribution limits based on earned income from January 1st to the date of death. The contribution must be made to the spousal plan within 60 days after December 31st of the year of death. This contribution could provide a valuable deduction to a deceased person who has a tax liability resulting from deemed dispositions that occur for tax purposes upon death.

The reality is that most families are not thinking about RRSPs in moments of bereavement. If spousal RRSP contributions are made early in January each year you'll ensure that, at the time of death, the contribution has already been made, and this will be one less thing to have to deal with.

What We Have Learned:
- *a contribution can be made to a spousal RRSP out of the assets of a deceased individual.*
- *the contribution is subject to the usual contribution limits and must be made in or before the year the surviving spouse turns age 71, and must be made within 60 days of December 31st of the year of death.*
- *avoid having to deal with RRSP contributions upon death by contributing in early January each year.*

Self-Directed RRSPs

LESSON 76

Move to a self-directed RRSP once your total plan assets reach $20,000.

RRSPs offered at many banks, life insurance companies, and mutual fund companies are generally not self-directed plans. That is, you cannot usually hold any investment you'd like inside the plan. Generally you can only hold the investments offered by the particular company. For example, if you have an RRSP at any of the major banks, you'll be able to hold that bank's mutual funds inside your RRSP, but you couldn't hold, say, shares of Bell Canada in the plan. This lack of flexibility and inability to diversify could limit the rate of return on your RRSP assets over the long-term. For this reason, we recommend that you move to a self-directed RRSP once your plan assets reach $20,000.

A self-directed RRSP must be established with a brokerage firm or another financial institution or company that offers them. You'll have more flexibility as to the type of investments held inside the plan. The investments held in the plan will be restricted to qualified investments, however there's lots to pick from (see lesson 63). Waiting until you have $20,000 makes sense for two reasons. First, the annual fee on a self-directed plan will range from $100 to $150, which is more than the fees under a non-self-directed plan. This higher fee will, in effect, reduce the return on your RRSP assets, but where your assets are $20,000 or more, the effect on your overall rate of return becomes very small. Second, having $20,000 or more inside your plan will allow for proper diversification of your investments (it's easier to avoid the "all eggs in one basket" problem).

If you get nervous about the idea of controlling what investments are held inside your self-directed plan, perhaps because you don't know much about investing, there's a simple solution. Open your self-directed plan with a reputable investment broker. A broker will help to manage what investments are held inside your RRSP, and can give you that peace of mind that comes when your investments are being looked after. Your C.A. can recommend a good investment broker.

What We Have Learned:
- *a self-directed RRSP is more flexible and offers better diversification than other RRSPs because you can hold any qualified investment of your choice inside the plan.*
- *once your RRSP assets reach $20,000 open a self-directed plan.*
- *use the advice of a reputable investment broker if you're not comfortable choosing your own investments.*

Investing Inside Your RRSP

LESSON 77

Avoid non-qualified investments inside your RRSP.

We've already talked briefly about qualified investments for your RRSP (see lesson 63 for a list). The issue of non-qualified investments is generally a concern only when you have a self-directed RRSP, otherwise the company administering your RRSP will generally only offer qualifying investments. Even where your plan is self-directed, the trust company is required to inform you of any income inclusions that result from non-qualifying investments. Where you've invested in non-qualifying assets inside your plan, there are three potential consequences: (1) you could be subject to penalty taxes where you've exceeded the foreign content limits (to be discussed in lesson 78), (2) income earned on non-qualifying investments inside your RRSP will be subject to tax at the highest marginal tax rate, and (3) the cost of non-qualified investments will be included in your income in the year of purchase. By the way, regarding point number 2, any capital gains earned inside your RRSP on non-qualified investments will be *fully* taxed, not merely 75% taxable as is usually the case.

What We Have Learned:
- *there are three potential consequences to holding non-qualified investments inside your RRSP: (1) you could be subject to penalty taxes, (2) income earned on the investments inside your RRSP will be fully taxed at the highest marginal rate, and (3) the cost of the investment will be included in your income in the year you purchased it.*

LESSON 78

Maximize the foreign content inside your RRSP.

The taxman will only allow a certain portion of your RRSP to be invested in qualified foreign investments. Since 1994 this portion has been, and continues to be, 20% of the cost of all investments inside your RRSP. Be careful – if you exceed this limit, you'll face penalty taxes calculated as 1% per month of the excess amount invested in foreign securities. The penalty will be applied each month until you withdraw the excess foreign content. While you need to monitor how much foreign content is in your plan (most companies administering your RRSP will do this for you) to ensure you don't exceed the 20% limit, you should certainly be maximizing your foreign content. There are three good reason for this.

Maximize Returns
Foreign securities have historically offered higher returns over the long term than Canadian securities. For example, $1000 invested in the TSE 300 (a Toronto stock index) in 1986 would be worth $2,193 today, whereas $1,000 invested in the S&P 500 (a U.S. stock index) would be worth $4,042 today – significantly higher.

Expand Selection

Canadian securities represent about 2% of the total securities available world-wide. This is a remarkably small proportion, and by restricting yourself to Canadian securities you'll undoubtedly be overlooking excellent opportunities elsewhere.

Reduce Exposure to Volatile or Stagnant Markets

Holding the maximum foreign content will reduce your exposure to the volatility of Canadian securities resulting from political uncertainty (i.e. the Quebec separation issue) and significant national debt. In addition, there are times when the Canadian economy is moving in a direction that could limit investment returns. For example, when interest rates are low and begin to rise, it may be difficult to find a good place to park your money in Canada. Since economies around the world move in different directions at different times, there may be good opportunities elsewhere even when markets in Canada become volatile or stagnant.

There are some creative, and perfectly legal, ways to increase your foreign content above the 20% limit provided by statute. Consider the stories of Barry and Jill.

Barry Buys Bonds

Barry wanted to increase the foreign content inside his RRSP above 20%, so he approached his investment advisor. His advisor suggested investing in Canadian Foreign-Pay bonds. These are bonds issued by Canadian federal and provincial agencies, such as utilities, that are denominated in foreign currencies. Barry's advisor suggested that the easiest way to make this investment was through a mutual fund. Many Canadian-based international bond funds invest in foreign markets by purchasing these bonds. Barry was especially happy that these bonds are not considered foreign content inside his RRSP, and still provide diversification away from Canada.

Jill's Clever Idea

Jill also decided to maximize her foreign content, but went about it a different way. Jill had invested in Canadian securities with a cost of $800, and in foreign securities with a cost of $200, for a total cost of $1,000 inside her RRSP, so that she was at her 20% foreign content limit. The Canadian securities increased in value to $1,200. She sold the Canadian securities for $1,200 and immediately bought them back for the same *amount. There was no tax on the sale since it happened inside her RRSP, and she now has a new cost for her Canadian securities of $1,200. The total cost inside her RRSP is now $1,200 Canadian plus $200 foreign, for a total of $1,400. Her foreign content is now just 14.3% ($200 out of $1,400). Jill then purchased $100 of foreign securities to bring her foreign content back up to 20% of her total cost. Jill has successfully increased her foreign content.*

You'll make it easier to invest in foreign content if you have just one RRSP, as opposed to many separate RRSP accounts. Why? Because the 20% limit is "per RRSP", and you'll need to have Canadian content in your RRSP before you can calculate your allowable foreign content. By putting all your Canadian content in a single RRSP basket you'll maximize the amount of foreign content that can be held in one place, which will make purchasing the foreign securities that much easier.

One last thing. Many mutual fund companies and investment brokers will monitor your foreign content for you and will automatically transfer some of your money to Canadian investments once you're over the 20% foreign limit. To make this job easier, they may make the 20% calculation based on the *current value* of your investments rather than the *original cost* – be sure to monitor this since you could end up with less foreign content than you're entitled to.

What We Have Learned:

- *foreign content inside your RRSP is limited to 20% of the cost of the assets inside your plan.*
- *penalties of 1% per month are levied on excess foreign content.*
- *there are three good reasons to maximize your foreign content: you'll maximize returns, expand your selection, and reduce your exposure to volatile or stagnant markets.*
- *there are creative and legal ways to effectively increase your foreign content above the 20% statutory limit.*
- *investing in foreign content will be easier when you have just one RRSP.*

LESSON 79

Hold interest-bearing investments inside your RRSP.

Interest income has its pros and cons. On the pro side, the investments paying you interest are generally conservative, so there's little chance that you'll lose any capital (your original investment). On the con side, interest is taxed at a higher rate than dividends or capital gains. Refer to Appendix 2 at the back of the book for marginal tax rates on different types of income. Holding interest-bearing investments inside your RRSP, however, won't hurt you from a tax point of view since income inside your RRSP is not taxed until you withdraw it. Refer to lesson 40 for a talk on earning interest versus dividends and capital gains inside your RRSP.

What We Have Learned:

• *interest income is taxed at a higher rate than dividends or capital gains, and should be earned inside your RRSP to reduce and defer taxable income.*

LESSON 80

Hold shares or equity mutual funds inside your RRSP to maximize returns.

Some people believe that only interest-bearing investments should be held inside an RRSP. Unfortunately, this overlooks one very important fact: equity investments have consistently earned higher *real* returns (returns after inflation is factored in) over the long-term than interest-bearing investments. Real returns inside your RRSP should be your most important consideration since all funds withdrawn from your RRSP are taxed at the same rate (refer to lesson 40) suggesting that taxes are not an issue when investing inside your RRSP. Since your RRSP is a long-term investment vehicle, and equities earn higher real returns over the long-term, you'll earn more in your plan by holding at least a portion of your assets in equities – that is, primarily shares and equity mutual funds.

What We Have Learned:
- *shares and equity mutual funds will provide higher returns over the long-term than interest-bearing investments, and therefore should be included in a well-balanced RRSP.*

LESSON 81

Maximize your CDIC insurance protection by investing at more than one financial institution.

The *Canada Deposit Insurance Corporation (CDIC)* has been kind enough to provide you with protection in the event your financial institution should go bankrupt. Not all of your investments will be protected. Investments that qualify for protection include savings and chequing accounts, and GICs or term deposits that are redeemable within five years. The following investments are not covered: foreign currency deposits or foreign denominated GICs, and mutual funds. The coverage available to you is $60,000 per institution. Once your RRSP, or non-registered investments for that matter, exceed $60,000 in one account, consider opening another account at another institution to multiply your protection. You may be able to multiply your protection at any one institution by opening a second or third account under a different name, for example jointly with your spouse or in trust for your children.

The CDIC insurance is purchased for you buy your financial institution. You pay for it indirectly through lower interest rates on your GICs and other insured investments. But what if you own an investment worth, say, $100,000? You're accepting a lower interest rate on the full $100,000 (to pay for the CDIC insurance), but only $60,000 of that investment is protected by the insurance – a bad deal if there ever was one. Try negotiating with your bank for an additional 1/8th or 1/4 of a percent interest on your large investments. Typically, your ability to bargain will begin on investments of $100,000 or more.

What We Have Learned:
- *you're entitled to $60,000 of insurance protection from the CDIC for each of your financial institutions.*

- *not all investments are covered by the insurance.*
- *consider multiplying your coverage by opening new accounts when your investment reaches $60,000 in any single account.*
- *negotiate higher rates of interest on your investments of $100,000 or more, otherwise you'll be paying for insurance protection that you're not getting.*

Getting Money Out Of Your RRSP

What goes in, must come out. The money inside your RRSP won't stay there forever, and when it does come out (and there are a number of situations when it might) it will be taxed – or so the theory goes. In actual fact, withdrawing from or collapsing your RRSP won't always give rise to tax right away, and in some cases, maybe never.

GETTING MONEY OUT: WHEN YOU RETIRE

LESSON 82

You have three options for your RRSP funds when you retire.

When you retire, you'll have to decide what to do with the many thousands of dollars that have accumulated inside your RRSP. You may decide to do nothing the day you retire, but by December 31st of the year you turn age 71 you'll have to make a decision since your plan will mature on that date and you'll have to close it down. There are three options to consider, but you don't have to choose one over the others; you can adopt a combination of these three alternatives if you want.

Registered Retirement Income Fund (RRIF)

A RRIF is a plan that is much like your RRSP. In fact, you can even hold the same investments in your RRIF that you've been holding inside your RRSP, and like an RRSP, income earned inside the RRIF compounds tax-free. The difference is that you cannot make deductible contributions to a RRIF, and you're required to withdraw a minimum amount from your RRIF each year, except in the year you establish the plan (no withdrawals are required in the first year).

Any amounts withdrawn are taxable in the year of withdrawal. Regarding transfers, funds can be moved from one RRIF to another on a tax-free basis, and as with RRSPs, you can have more than one RRIF if you'd like.

The minimum withdrawal each year is based on the amount still in the plan at the start of the year, and is a fixed percentage of that opening balance. The fixed percentage required to be withdrawn is determined by the government and set out in their regulations. See Appendix 6 at the back of the book for these minimum withdrawal percentages. One last point: you're able to use your spouse's age to calculate the minimum withdrawal. The choice to do this must be made before your first withdrawal from the RRIF. It always makes sense to use the age of the younger spouse since this will result in a lower minimum withdrawal amount each year, and therefore will provide a longer tax deferral. Besides, you can always withdraw more than the minimum if you'd like – in fact, you could withdraw the whole RRIF if you wanted to (but we wouldn't recommend this).

A quick note about Life Income Funds (LIFs). These plans operate under the same rules as RRIFs. Where your retirement income is sitting in a registered pension plan or a locked-in RRSP you may not be eligible to roll the funds into a RRIF when your plan matures since the funds are subject to certain locked-in provisions (see lesson 65). An alternative is a LIF. The primary differences between a RRIF and a LIF are that (1) a LIF must be closed and converted to an annuity on or before December 31st of the year you turn 80 years of age, and (2) LIFs are available across Canada, except in Prince Edward Island, Newfoundland, the Yukon, and the Northwest Territories.

The Annuity Alternative

An annuity is simply a stream of payments that is guaranteed to be paid to you over a certain time. The issuer of the annuity is generally a life insurance company. There are different types of annuities, but a *life annuity* is most common, and will pay you a fixed amount each month until you die.

The benefit of an annuity is the peace of mind that income will continue to be paid to you until death. With a RRIF, on the other hand, you may out-live your investments since a portion must be paid out to you each year. The main drawbacks to an annuity are that, unlike a RRIF, you have no control over your investments, and you generally won't be able to withdraw lump-sums of money. If security is more important than control over the management of your investments, an annuity might be for you. If you choose the annuity alternative, you'll want to maximize the interest rate paid by the annuity. So, don't wait until the last minute (the year you turn 71) to buy an annuity since you'll be forced to accept the going interest rate at that time. Buying the annuity a few years earlier if interest rates are high may be to your benefit.

Lump-Sum Withdrawal

You might decide to withdraw a portion of your RRSP funds upon retirement as a lump-sum amount rather than rolling your full RRSP into a RRIF or an annuity. You'll be taxed on any lump-sum withdrawals in the year you take the money out of the plan, and so we don't recommend that you take all your RRSP funds upon retirement as a lump-sum. It makes much more sense to defer taxes even longer by using a RRIF or an annuity.

What We Have Learned:

• *your RRSP will mature by December 31st of the year you turn age 71, and you must therefore decide what to do with your RRSP funds by that time.*

• *there are three options for the funds in your maturing RRSP: invest in a RRIF, an annuity, or take the funds as a lump-sum payment.*

LESSON 83

Take advantage of the $1,000 pension credit.

The taxman has been generous enough to provide a $1,000 credit to those who have received qualifying pension income in any year. The actual taxes saved as a result of this credit will be about $270, varying slightly from province to province. You'd be wise to report at least $1,000 of pension income (and your RRSP withdrawals may qualify) on your return to take advantage of this credit where possible. Where you've received less than $1,000 in pension income, your credit will be limited to 27% of that income. It's only *qualifying* pension income that will entitle you to this credit, and qualifying income will differ for those 65 years of age and better and those under 65.

You've Reached Age 65

For those who are 65 in the year, the pension income that qualifies for the credit is as follows: an annuity out of or under a superannuation or pension fund or plan, an annuity out of an RRSP, a payment out of a RRIF, an annuity payment out of a DPSP, the income portion of any annuity payment, and the income from an income-averaging annuity contract.

Not Yet 65 Years

If you're under age 65, you'll still be entitled to the pension credit for the following types of income: life annuity payments from a superannuation or pension plan (but not lump-sum payments), annuity payments arising from the death of your spouse out of an RRSP, RRIF, DPSP and other specified plans (including foreign government pension plans – U.S. social security for example), and the income portion of any annuity payment arising from the death of your spouse.

Obviously, the ability to claim the pension credit is more difficult if you're not yet 65 years of age. Try this idea: use some RRSP funds to buy a life annuity that will pay out $1,000 each year. The annuity will qualify as income eligible for the credit, so it will be largely tax-free. The transfer of these RRSP funds to the life annuity can be done on a tax-free basis.

You'll notice that certain payments have been left out above and won't entitle you to the pension credit. Most notably these include: Old Age Security (OAS) payments, and amounts under the Canada Pension Plan (CPP). By the way, you might remember from lesson 29, point 14 that the pension credit can be transferred to your spouse to be used by him or her if you're not able to benefit from it.

What We Have Learned:

- *certain types of pension income will entitle you to the $1,000 pension credit.*
- *take advantage of the credit by reporting at least $1,000 of qualifying pension income where possible; purchase a life annuity paying out $1,000 a year to make this easy.*

• *the pension credit can be transferred to your spouse where you're
not able to benefit from it and your spouse has qualifying income.*

GETTING MONEY OUT: FOR A HOME PURCHASE

LESSON 84

$▸$

***Consider using RRSP funds for a home
purchase – but not always.***

Back in 1992 the government introduced the *Home Buyers' Plan*
(HBP) to permit Canadians access to RRSP funds for the purpose of
buying a home. The plan can be useful to some home buyers, but
may not always make sense. Generally, where you have 35 or more
years to go before you retire, you'll be better off not using RRSP
funds toward a home purchase. The reason for this is straight forward. When you withdraw funds from your RRSP under the plan,
you'll lose the benefit of the tax-free growth those funds could have
earned over your years until retirement. The further away retirement
is, the more tax-free growth you'll lose. Thirty five years to go is
enough time that, in most cases, you'll be better off leaving the
money inside your RRSP. If you do decide to take advantage of the
HBP, there are things you need to know about the plan.

Withdrawing From Your RRSP
You and your spouse, where you have one, will be able to withdraw
up to $20,000 each from your respective RRSPs to put toward a
home purchase as long as neither you nor your spouse have owned
a home in the last 4 years. You may still be eligible for the plan if
your spouse has owned a home in the last four years that was not
your principal residence while you were married or in a common
law relationship. Further, you're only eligible for the plan once in a
lifetime, so if you've used it before, you won't be able to again.

Once you've withdrawn funds from your RRSP (use form T1036
for this), your home must be purchased, that is, the transaction must
be closed, before October 1st of the following year (the *completion
date*). So, a withdrawal in 1996 means you must close a home purchase before October 1, 1997. An extension may be possible in some
cases, and if you fail to acquire a home by the completion date, you

can put your funds back into your RRSP by December 31st of that year without a penalty. A qualifying home is any home located in Canada, or a share of the capital stock of a co-operative housing corporation in Canada. Finally, the home you acquire must be used by you as your principal residence within 12 months of purchasing it. [Note: this area of tax law has gone through a number of changes over the past few years, so if you took advantage of the HBP in 1992 or 1993 you'll be subject to slightly different rules.]

Repaying the Money

Any money withdrawn from your RRSP under the HBP has to be paid back in equal instalments over a 15 year period. The first instalment commences with the second year following the withdrawal, and you're given 60 days following the end of that year to make the required payment back to your RRSP. For example, a withdrawal in 1996 will require instalments to begin in 1998, but as with regular RRSP contributions, you'll have until March 1, 1999 (60 days after year end) to start making those instalments. If you miss an instalment, or pay less than the required amount, the shortfall will be a taxable RRSP withdrawal to you. Lastly, you can, if you'd like, repay more than the minimum instalment to your RRSP each year – if you do this, all future payments will be amended (reduced) to reflect the fact that the amount borrowed is closer to being fully repaid.

RRSP Contributions

The HBP rules were designed to allow access to funds already inside your RRSP, and so the rules won't allow you to make a contribution to your RRSP, withdraw the funds within 90 days to buy a home, and then claim a deduction for the contribution. Specifically, where you've made an RRSP contribution within the 90 days immediately prior to your HBP withdrawal, you won't be allowed a deduction for that contribution to the extent that the contribution is greater than the balance inside your RRSP after the withdrawal. To ensure a deductible contribution, make sure the funds sit inside your RRSP for more than 90 days before making your withdrawal.

What We Have Learned:

- *the Home Buyers' Plan allows a first-time home buyer use of up to $20,000 of RRSP funds for the purchase of a home; repayment must be made over 15 years.*

- *the plan may be worthwhile unless you have 35 years or more until retirement, in which case it won't usually be beneficial.*
- *there are many rules to respect under the plan and these should be understood before using it.*

GETTING MONEY OUT: FOR PERSONAL USE

There are times when you might want to access the funds inside your RRSP to cover cash shortfalls, to invest in business opportunities, or for other reasons. There are a few ways of doing this, and some on a tax-free basis. Before we give you any ideas, it's worth mentioning the drawbacks of taking money out of your plan for other uses. There are two good reasons you might not want to touch the funds inside your RRSP. First, there's the possibility that the withdrawal will be taxable. In fact, where your RRSP withdrawal plus other income exceeds $6,456 in 1996, a withdrawal will likely give rise to some tax. Second, you'll lose the tax-free compounding that you could have earned by leaving the funds inside the plan. The tax-free growth lost could be significant.

Amount of Withdrawal	RRSP Growth Lost Based on Years Until Retirement		
	10 yrs	20 yrs	30 yrs
$ 1,000	$ 2,594	$ 6,727	$ 17,449
3,000	7,781	20,182	52,348
5,000	12,969	33,637	87,247
7,000	18,156	47,092	122,146
10,000	25,937	67,275	174,494

Note: assumes an annual average rate of return of 10% inside your RRSP.

If you're still intent on using your RRSP savings for other things, here are a few ways of doing it.

LESSON 85

Withdraw RRSP funds during periods of no or low income.

At certain times in your life you might find yourself with little or no income in a given year. Maybe you're unemployed, or on disability leave without pay. Perhaps you've just had a child and spend most of your time at home, or you're in the process of getting a business up and running but haven't started making money yet. The financial strain in these times can be helped by making use of money in your RRSP, and line 300 on your tax return can make it happen tax-free.

On line 300 of your return you'll find a tax credit called your *basic personal amount*. For 1996 this amount is $6,456, and every Canadian receives a federal tax credit equal to 17% of $6,456, or $1,098.[1] Having this credit available means that you can earn up to $6,456 in 1996 without paying a cent of tax. In a year where your income is low, simply withdraw enough money from your RRSP to top up your income to the basic personal amount ($6,456 in 1996) and the money is tax-free. We should mention that when you make withdrawals from your RRSP, your financial institution will withhold 10% (on withdrawals of $5,000 or less) and send it to the taxman. You'll get the cash back when you file your tax return if your income is under the basic personal amount.

When you decide to withdraw funds from a spousal RRSP be aware that the money might be taxed in the hands of the contributor, and not the annuitant spouse, where contributions were made in the year of withdrawal or the preceding two years. Refer back to lessons 72 and 73 for more details.

What We Have Learned:

- *your RRSP can provide income during periods of no or low income.*
- *provided your total income is under $6,456 in 1996 the money will come out of your RRSP tax-free, and tax withheld by your*

---

[1] The basic personal amount is increased in any year that inflation is over 3%. The last increase was in 1992. If the amount had been indexed for inflation each year since 1992, it would be $7,788 in 1996. The fact that the amount has not increased effectively means that we have experienced a tax increase – a silent tax grab.

financial institution upon withdrawal will be refunded, in this case, when you file your tax return.

• *beware of possible attribution on withdrawals from a spousal RRSP.*

LESSON 86

Make RRSP withdrawals in increments of $5,000 or less.

As mentioned in the last lesson, when you withdraw money from your RRSP, your financial institution is required to withhold tax and remit it to Revenue Canada, much like income tax deducted from your pay at work. There's really no way of getting around this. If your income is low enough for the year, you may get all or a portion of the tax back when you file your tax return in April. You can, however, minimize the tax withheld when you make your withdrawals by withdrawing in increments of $5,000 or less. The reason for this is that the tax withheld is only 10% on withdrawals of $5,000 or less, but 20% on withdrawals between $5,000 and $15,000, and 30% on withdrawals over $15,000 (the rates are 18%, 30% and 35% respectively in Quebec). The less withholding tax you pay, the more money in your pocket to use for other things.

Keep in mind that RRSP withdrawals are taxable, and so you could end up owing money in April if your income (including the RRSP withdrawals) is high enough. The 10% tax withheld by your financial institution is never sufficient to cover your tax liability if the whole withdrawal is taxable since the lowest marginal tax rate is about 25%, depending on your province (see Appendix 2).

What We Have Learned:
• *RRSP withdrawals are subject to withholding tax at your financial institution.*
• *this withholding tax can be minimized by withdrawing funds in increments of $5,000.*
• *be aware that you could end up owing money when you file your tax return if your income, including RRSP withdrawals, is high enough and the 10% tax withheld by your financial institution was insufficient.*

LESSON 87

Consider investing in your own mortgage with funds inside your RRSP.

There may be times when it makes sense to use funds inside your RRSP to provide a mortgage to yourself for any number of reasons – investing in your business, or to buy a new home, for example. The mortgage will be secured by real estate owned by you. Rather than borrowing from a financial institution, you can use the funds inside your self-directed RRSP to provide the necessary cash, and mortgage payments would then be made to your RRSP rather than to your bank, trust company, or other institution. As a general rule, you need to have substantial savings in your RRSP to make this worthwhile. We don't recommend the idea unless you're going to be borrowing at least $100,000 from your RRSP. To be in a position to do this, you may want at least $200,000 in your RRSP to limit the mortgage to 50% of your total RRSP. You could invest more than 50% in your mortgage, but it's important that your investments be properly diversified, so we'd recommend visiting a qualified financial planner (an RFP for example) for advice.

Ken and Leslie's Mortgage
Ken and Leslie have substantial savings in their self-directed RRSP, and decided to invest those funds in a mortgage on their dream home rather than going to their bank for the money. They went through all the paperwork (about $3,000 worth) necessary to set up a $100,000 mortgage at a rate of 9%. This means that those funds inside the RRSP are now earning a rate of return of 9% annually – or so they thought. Ken and Leslie paid one-time fees of about $3,000 to set up the mortgage, and are paying an annual fee of about $250 each year to the trust company administering the RRSP. These fees effectively reduce the rate of return on the RRSP funds to 8.36% each year from the 9% stated in the mortgage documentation. If Ken and Leslie had borrowed just $50,000 from their RRSP, the fees would reduce the rate of return on those RRSP funds to about 7.74% each year. The less money they borrow from their RRSP, the worse the rate of return inside their RRSP becomes due to the one-time set-up and annual fees. At some point, the rate of return inside the plan will become low

enough that they would be better off putting their RRSP funds into a different investment that will pay a higher return.

If you're in a position to invest $100,000 of your RRSP funds in a mortgage on your home or other property, there are other things to consider before you take the plunge. Most importantly, visit a tax professional first.

The One-Time Costs To Consider

When you invest RRSP funds in a mortgage to yourself, it's called a *non-arm's-length* mortgage. A mortgage of this type must be insured by the Canadian Mortgage and Housing Corporation (CMHC) which will be a one-time cost to you between 0.5% and 2.5% of all mortgage principal amounts on the home, including previous mortgages, depending on what percentage the mortgages are of your property's value. Your trust company administering the plan will charge a one-time set up fee of about $200 (shop around), and your lawyer will want a fee to prepare the mortgage documentation and to register the mortgage. The CMHC will also require an appraisal done on the property which could cost $200 or more. The total one-time fees to set up a mortgage will vary, but could be $3,000 to $5,000. In addition to these one-time costs, there will be an annual administration fee charged by your trust company which could be $250 or more each year.

Commercial Rate of Interest

Any time you're dealing with a non-arm's-length mortgage held inside your RRSP, there's the requirement that the rate of interest charged be consistent with commercial rates available at your financial institution. For this reason, you might want to wait until interest rates are relatively high before you invest RRSP funds in a mortgage. This will maximize the rate of return inside your RRSP.

Is This Really A Great Idea?

First, it's important to realize that using your RRSP funds to provide a mortgage won't save you interest costs. Don't forget, whether you're borrowing from the bank, or your RRSP, you still have to make interest payments – it's just that one provides interest to your RRSP while the other provides interest to your bank. Isn't it better to pay interest to yourself than to the bank? From a peace-of-mind perspective perhaps, but not necessarily from a financial perspective.

To see this, let's consider what happens inside, and outside your RRSP. First, outside your RRSP. You're paying interest regardless of who you borrow from, the bank or your RRSP – end of story. Now, consider what happens inside your RRSP. All you're doing is moving those funds in your plan from one investment to another investment – your mortgage. When you invest in your own mortgage you give up the income you could have earned by investing in other things. If the rate of return offered by the mortgage is lower than what your RRSP could have earned elsewhere, your RRSP might actually be worse off. So why bother with this idea? The following situations might indicate that it's worthwhile doing, but even in these scenarios there may be reasons not to:

- you're not able to get financing from a financial institution.
- you simply don't want to deal with a financial institution.
- the rate on the mortgage is higher than the return you could earn elsewhere.
- the mortgage interest will be deductible since you're running a business from home.

What We Have Learned:

- *it may make sense to provide a mortgage to yourself with the funds in your self-directed RRSP in four situations: you can't get financing from an institution, you don't want to deal with an institution, the mortgage rate is higher than the return you could earn elsewhere, or the mortgage interest will be deductible.*
- *your mortgage should be for at least $100,000 but should still allow for proper diversification of your assets.*
- *seek professional advice before trying this idea.*

GETTING MONEY OUT: WHEN YOU LEAVE CANADA

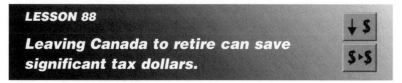

LESSON 88

Leaving Canada to retire can save significant tax dollars.

If you should decide that, for one reason or another, you'd like to leave Canada to spend the rest of your days in the United States or elsewhere, don't rush to collapse your RRSP! Generally, you'll save tax dollars by leaving your RRSP intact and withdrawing your money from the plan after you become a resident elsewhere. The reason for this is that the only tax you'll pay in Canada on your RRSP withdrawals once you've given up Canadian residency is, at most, a withholding tax of 25%, which is often reduced to 15% or less under tax treaties with other countries. The table below shows those countries whose treaties with Canada provide the most favourable tax treatment on payments out of an RRSP. Notice that where you take up residency in the Netherlands, the amount of tax withheld by Canada on any payments out of your RRSP will be *nil* – that's right, zero. The amount of tax withheld in any country will depend on whether the payment is a periodic or lump-sum payment out of your plan. As for the funds in your registered pension plan at work, the withholding tax rates are at least as favourable as these, and sometimes better, depending on the country.

	Country	Periodic Payments	Lump-Sum Payments
	CANADIAN WITHHOLDING TAX ON RRSP WITHDRAWALS BY COUNTRY OF RESIDENCE		
	Australia	15	25
	Barbados	15	25
(2)	Denmark	Nil	25
	Finland	Nil	25
	Germany	15	25
(2)	Ireland	Nil	15
	Netherlands	Nil	Nil
(1)	New Zealand	Nil/15	Nil/25
(2)	Norway	Nil	25
	Trinidad & Tobago	Nil	25
	United States	15	25

(1) First $10,000 is tax-free, then 15% on periodic and 25% on lump-sum payments.

(2) Treaty with this country is currently being renegotiated.

Rather than paying withholding tax in Canada when you make RRSP withdrawals from another country, you can elect to file a Canadian tax return and report your RRSP withdrawals as taxable income. If this income represents at least 50% of your total world-wide income, you'll be eligible to claim a number of deductions and personal tax credits on your Canadian return. In this situation you might be able to create an even better effective tax rate than the 15% or other withholding rate that applies. Generally, your withdrawals will have to be under $30,000 each year to have a chance at beating any withholding tax rate.

Giving Up Residency

In order to take advantage of the low withholding tax rates we've been talking about you'll have to give up Canadian residency because individuals are taxed in Canada if they are considered *residents* of Canada (citizenship is not relevant as it is in the U.S.). Who is a resident of Canada? The tax law doesn't provide a definition – it's really a question of a series of facts.

There are steps you can take to ensure that you've made a clean break from Canada, and we recommend that you visit a tax professional to make sure you leave Canada properly. Some steps you should take to give up residency include: (1) sell your home and cottage, (2) close bank and other accounts, (3) give up memberships in clubs and organizations, (4) avoid visits to Canada of long duration (if you stay in Canada for 183 days or more in any year you'll be deemed a resident of Canada), (5) establish residency elsewhere, and the list goes on. No single fact will cause you to be a resident of Canada – all facts will have to be considered together.

Leaving for the United States

In addition to the withholding tax payable to Canada on RRSP withdrawals, you'll also be taxed in your new country of residence on the income. The United States, however, provides some attractive tax savings. The U.S. will only tax you on income earned inside your RRSP from the date you take up residence in the U.S. This means that the book value (original cost) of your RRSP on the day you arrive in the U.S. can be taken out tax-free down there. The income you earn inside your RRSP after arriving in the U.S. will be taxable each year, although it's still sheltered from tax in Canada until withdrawn from the plan. Fortunately, an election is available in the U.S.

to defer tax on the income growing inside your RRSP. The election must be made every year when you file your tax return in the U.S., and it's very important that you *do not forget to file this election*. The benefits are too great to ignore.

Paul Moves South

Last year, Paul decided to move to the U.S. because of a job opportunity he couldn't pass up. When he left, he had an RRSP with a book value of $200,000. This $200,000 is not taxable in the U.S. This year, those RRSP funds earned $20,000 in income which is taxable in the U.S. unless an election is filed. Paul filed the required election, and will do this every year to ensure he pays no tax until the funds are withdrawn from his RRSP. Paul will benefit in two important ways for filing this election: (1) he will defer tax in the U.S. on the income growing inside his RRSP, and (2) he'll be able to match the timing of taxation in the U.S. with the timing in Canada – that is, he won't be taxed in either country until he makes withdrawals. This matching is important since he'll be able to claim a foreign tax credit in the U.S. for the withholding taxes he'll pay in Canada. This credit will quite probably offset his tax liability in the U.S. The end result is that the only tax he'll likely pay is the 15% withholding tax in Canada. If he had stayed in Canada and made his RRSP withdrawals, his tax could have been as high as 54%.

Remember that the U.S. will eventually tax any income or realized capital gains earned inside your RRSP from the time you become a U.S. resident. As a result, we recommend that you consider selling (and perhaps buying back) any investments inside your RRSP that have accrued capital gains before you leave Canada. Doing this will provide you with a "step-up" in the book value of your RRSP which can be taken out tax-free in the U.S.

If you sell these investments after you leave, the U.S. will tax you on any gains eventually. Selling them beforehand might not make much of a difference later since, as Paul's story shows, the tax you pay in the U.S. could be very small. For some people, however, this idea could save considerable taxes. We'd like to mention again that there are other countries around the world that do not levy taxes on investment and pension income earned elsewhere, so your RRSP income could grow and be withdrawn without any tax at all except the Canadian withholding taxes payable on withdrawals.

If you're thinking of leaving Canada, we recommend that you visit a tax professional to find out the implications of moving abroad.

What We Have Learned:

- *don't collapse your RRSP before leaving Canada since the withholding tax you'll pay later will likely be less than the tax payable as a resident of Canada.*
- *becoming a resident of the United States has some real tax advantages as far as accessing your RRSP funds at a low tax rate is concerned.*
- *if you take up residence in the U.S., be sure to file an election each year to defer taxation of the income growing inside your RRSP.*
- *see a tax professional if you're thinking of moving abroad.*

Self-Employment 8

Becoming Self-Employed

The concept of employment has changed in Canada over the past few years, and it's safe to say that we'll never view employment quite the same again. The word employment was once synonymous with words such as *long-term, security, loyalty,* and *lifetime.* The effects of the recession of the early 1990s, however, are still being felt, and the new view of employment that has emerged is more closely associated with terms like *uncertain, career-change, part-time,* and *every-man-for-himself.* It can be a frightening time for some, but it's also an opportunity for those with initiative and skills or knowledge to offer.

Many people have turned to self-employment to either supplement their employment income, or in some cases, to replace it altogether. Full-time self-employment is not for everyone – are you cut out for it? There's no single skill or quality you'll need, but the following are common among the successfully self-employed: specific and well-established skills or knowledge, a high energy level, the willingness to work long hours and accept risks, and sufficient start-up money. If this doesn't sound like you, part-time self-employment is an excellent alternative. Self-employment brings the opportunity for greater income, control over your own time, a sense of accomplishment, and a multiplication of tax planning opportunities. It's this last benefit we'd like to talk about here.

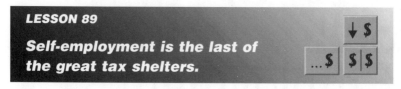

LESSON 89

Self-employment is the last of the great tax shelters.

While there are still a variety of ways to reduce your tax bill, and we've introduced many of them already, nothing is as attractive as self-employment. What's so great about it? As a self-employed tax-payer you're given tax breaks that employees can only dream of. If you'll remember back to our discussion on deductions available to employees in lesson 8, you'll recall that those deductions are limited to a few very specific situations. A business, on the other hand, is allowed to take a deduction for any expense[2] incurred for the purpose of gaining or producing income from the business, with some exceptions.

In other words, the Income Tax Act will not allow employees to claim any deductions except for those few things listed, while the Act allows businesses to claim deductions for anything the business considers necessary, with a few exceptions.

A True Story

This story is true – believe it or not. Heavy metal rock bands are usually known for their "scary" on-stage costumes. The taxpayers in question were members of a Canadian heavy metal band, and they spent "big" dollars on their clothing for performances. They deducted the cost of the clothing on their personal tax returns. Revenue Canada disallowed the deductions, as is usually the case for clothing, because there's usually a definite personal benefit to owning the clothing despite the fact that it might be worn for business purposes as well. The accountant for the band sent a picture of the band in their performance garb to the taxman and attached a note: "Would you wear this kind of clothing to the grocery store?" The taxman obviously concluded that there could be no personal benefit to owning the clothes because the deduction was allowed.

The point to remember: any costs incurred for the purpose of earning business income can be deducted. Employees don't have this

---

[2]   The types of expenses that are deductible are only limited by your imagination and subject to a reasonableness test. Ask yourself: can the costs be reasonably considered to have been incurred to produce income from the business? If so, deduct them. Note: there are certain expenses that are specifically disallowed.

luxury of deductions. Earning self-employment income is simply a way of increasing your deductions, thereby reducing your taxable income (the first pillar of tax planning), and paying less tax as a result.

What We Have Learned:
• *businesses are allowed any deductions incurred for the purpose of earning business income, with some exceptions.*
• *employees are not allowed any deductions against income, with some exceptions.*
• *there's a big difference between the two, and business (self-employment) income is very attractive as a result.*

LESSON 90

Arrange to be a consultant rather than an employee.

Since business income is so attractive due to the many deductions available, one of your tax planning objectives should be to earn this type of income. Consider approaching your employer to terminate your employee relationship and establish a consulting relationship instead (many corporations are doing this with retired or surplus employees). There's a pitfall you'll have to watch for if you're going to do this, but if you structure things right, you'll enjoy some significant write-offs against your income which we'll talk more about later. Here's the pitfall to watch for.

Laurie the Employee?
Laurie worked for Software Inc. for a few years. She is a programmer. Two years ago she quit her job and was re-hired on a contract basis and writes software for the company. She does most of her work at home but does spend time at Software Inc., especially for meetings. Revenue Canada audited Laurie last year and is investigating her relationship with Software Inc. aggressively. The taxman claims that she is actually an employee of Software Inc., and not a self-employed consultant. If she loses this battle, all the deductions she has claimed for the last two years will be disallowed (since employees are not allowed the deductions she has claimed) and she'll have a large tax liability. In addition, Software Inc. will

be on the hook for its share of her CPP, UIC, and provincial payroll taxes. She may have an argument that she is truly a consultant, but she could have avoided this mess by taking greater steps to ensure that her relationship was truly a consulting one.

The line between an employee and a consultant is not always a clear one. Revenue Canada doesn't really care if you *call* your relationship a consulting one. They will look at the facts of each case to make a determination. The following is a list of things the taxman will consider if he comes knocking at your door to check you out. No single item on this list will prove you're a self-employed consultant, but the more questions you can answer YES the better.

1. Do you control *when, where,* and *how* you do your work?
2. Are you economically independent of the company, meaning they are not your only source of income?
3. Are you able to work for other companies?
4. Do you have the power to hire employees or subcontractors that will report to you?
5. Do you assume any risks, supply any funds, or bear any liabilities in your activities?
6. Is there a foreseeable end to the project you're working on (as opposed to having a relationship that envisages an indefinite continuation of work)?
7. Do you provide your own supplies and equipment?
8. Are you ineligible for the same rights, privileges, and benefits as employees of the company?
9. Is the company able to survive without your services (as opposed to you being an integral part of the business)?
10. Do you issue invoices to the company and receive cheques (but are not issued a T4 or similar slip)?

The more questions you answered YES, the better chance that you have of claiming self-employment and all the deductions that go along with it. You must be sure to sign an agreement with the company outlining the nature, extent, and duration of your consulting work. If you do this, and take steps to answer the above questions with a YES, then you'll be in great shape. Keep in mind that, as a consultant, you won't have any recourse for wrongful dismissal if the company decides not to renew or simply terminates your contract.

What We Have Learned:
- *approach your employer and start a relationship as a consultant rather than an employee. This will open the door to many attractive deductions not otherwise available.*
- *be careful to ensure that your relationship is truly a consulting one by using the ten question checklist above.*
- *sign an agreement in writing to detail the nature, extent, and duration of your consulting arrangement.*

LESSON 91

Start a part-time business when you cannot become self-employed full time.

If your relationship with your employer just won't allow for you to become a consultant, and full-time self-employment isn't in the cards, you can still enjoy the benefits of self-employment by starting a part-time business. The most significant benefit of this idea is that the business will be eligible for write-offs that will not only shelter the income from your part-time business from tax, but could go further and shelter some of your employment and investment income from tax as well. This will happen where your part-time business generates a loss for tax purposes. It's important to note that a loss for tax purposes does not necessarily mean that the cash brought in by the business was less than the cash paid out, because some expenses are non-cash expenses, like the depreciation of assets (called capital cost allowance).

Revenue Canada has a requirement that you be in business to make a profit. This doesn't mean you have to show a profit every year, but you must have a reasonable expectation of profit in the foreseeable future. If you can demonstrate to the government that you expect to earn a profit in the next five to ten years you should be ok. To convince Revenue Canada that you're running a legitimate business, you should take certain steps such as: preparing a business plan, preparing forecasts for the next few years, registering your business name with your province, opening a separate bank account for the business, and advertising. Further, the likelihood of earning a profit will increase as you spend additional time in your part-time business, so showing Revenue Canada the number of hours spent in your pursuit could help your cause. The taxman is clamping down on basement businesses that aren't legitimate, so beware. Refer back to lesson 20 for more information.

What We Have Learned:
• *start a part-time business to make deductions available that could shelter not only your part-time income from tax, but income from your employment and investments as well.*
• *you must have a reasonable expectation of profit in the foreseeable future to be able to claim losses from a part-time business.*

Using Your Business To Save Taxes

As a self-employed consultant or part-time business owner, you'll be eligible for the many write-offs available to any business. While we couldn't possibly mention all the deductions that might be available to you, there are five common ones that are worth mentioning. Lessons 92 to 96 deal with these.

LESSON 92

↓ $

Claim Capital Cost Allowance on personal assets used in your business.

There are certain capital assets that you might purchase to enable you to earn business income. Capital assets are generally those that help you earn income over a period of years, like a car, computer, fax machine, photocopier, desk, or other furniture, to name a few. These capital assets are depreciable for tax purposes. If you use them partially for personal use, then only the business portion will be depreciable. Rather than taking a full deduction for these items in the year you buy them, Revenue Canada insists that you write them off over a period of years. This deduction each year is called *capital cost allowance (CCA)*, and is really a form of depreciation for tax purposes.

In a nutshell, your capital assets will be grouped into classes, and CCA will be claimed against the remaining balance (the Unclaimed Capital Cost) in the class each year, on a declining balance basis for most classes. Generally, only one half of the CCA otherwise allowed is permitted in the first year of ownership of an asset. The rules are complex and if you can't understand Revenue Canada's *Business and Professional Income Tax Guide*, then see a tax professional. See Appendix 7 at the back for a list of common CCA classes and rates.

The real benefit of CCA is that you're able to write-off the cost of assets that employees, even commissioned salespeople (see lesson 8, point 1), typically cannot. Sometimes these assets are things you'd buy for your home anyway – a computer for example – so taking a deduction for them and thereby sheltering income from tax is a real bonus. In addition, CCA is a discretionary deduction, so you don't have to claim it in years where you don't need the deduction – you can save it for years when you need it most. We recommend, where you've decided to buy capital assets, that you buy the assets and make them available for use in your business before year end rather than waiting until the next fiscal year. This will enable you to claim CCA on those assets a full year sooner.

What We Have Learned:
- *capital assets, even personal ones used in your business, can be written off over a period of years against income by claiming capital cost allowance (CCA).*
- *CCA is a discretionary deduction, so you can claim it in the years you need it most.*
- *buy assets before year end to enable a CCA claim a full year sooner.*
- *CCA calculations can be complex, so see a tax professional if you have trouble.*

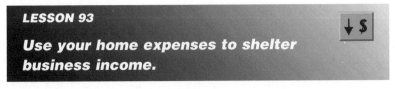

LESSON 93

Use your home expenses to shelter business income.

If you have a room or area in your home that has been set aside as an office for your consulting or other business, you can claim a portion of your recurring home expenses as a deduction provided (1) your home is your principal place of business, or (2) the office is used exclusively for the business and you meet clients, customers, or patients there on a regular and continuing basis. The deductible portion will usually depend on the size of your office in relation to the rest of your home. Here are some of the deductible expenses to claim.

DEDUCTIBLE HOME OFFICE EXPENSES

- rent (where you rent your home)
- mortgage interest
- property taxes
- heat, hydro, and water
- telephone
- repairs and maintenance (indoor and outdoor)
- home insurance

You can also claim CCA on the portion of your home used as an office, but we don't recommend it. Claiming CCA will cause problems when you later sell your home since Revenue Canada will take the view that the office portion of your home was not part of your principal residence (it was a business property), and this could result, among other things, in a taxable capital gain if your home has appreciated in value.

Expenses related to your office can only be used to bring your business income down to nil. You can't create or increase a loss to be applied against other types of income with your home expenses. As a result, if there are home office expenses that you cannot deduct, they can be carried forward to be used in any future year against income from your business. Be sure to keep track of and report these home office expenses, even where you don't expect much income for a few years – this way, you'll have the expenses available to offset that future income. Start reporting these expenses on your tax return in the first year you started thinking about beginning a business – this will maximize the expenses available for future use. One last point: it appears that home office expenses accumulated in one business can even be applied against income from another business later.

What We Have Learned:
- *claim expenses related to an office in your home where it's your principal place of business or you use the space exclusively to meet clients, customers, or patients.*
- *normally we do not recommend claiming capital cost allowance on your home.*
- *start reporting your home-office expenses as soon as you begin thinking about a home-based business and deduct them when you're finally earning profits.*

LESSON 94

Claim automobile expenses to shelter business income.

↓ $

You'll be able to deduct a portion of all your automobile costs where you use your car for business purposes. The portion deductible depends on the kilometres driven for business purposes. Technically, you're supposed to keep a log of all kilometres driven for business as evidence for your claim, but from a practical point of view, Revenue Canada rarely asks to see this information. It's up to you whether you want to chance making a claim without any support, but be prepared to have your deduction disallowed if the taxman comes asking for evidence. By the way, driving from home to your regular place of business is not considered business usage.

If your vehicle is used 50% for business, then one half of all vehicle expenses would be deductible. These costs include oil and gas, repairs, insurance, licence fees, washing costs, auto club costs, loan interest or lease costs, and capital cost allowance where you own the car. Your CCA claim for the vehicle will be based on a maximum cost of $24,000 plus GST and provincial sales tax (PST), even where the vehicle cost more than that. The maximum interest deductible on a vehicle loan is $300 per month, and the maximum lease cost deductible is $650 per month plus GST and PST.

Finally, where you have two or more cars, try to use one car strictly for business purposes and leave the others for personal use. This will maximize your allowable deductions.

What We Have Learned:
- *you'll be able to write-off the business portion of your vehicle costs; Revenue Canada has the right to ask to see a log of your business kilometres as evidence of business usage.*
- *costs that are deductible include oil and gas, repairs, insurance, licence fees, washing costs, auto club costs, loan interest or lease costs, and capital cost allowance.*
- *where you have more than one vehicle, try to use one exclusively for business purposes to maximize your deductions.*

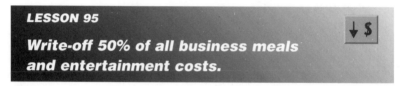

LESSON 95

Write-off 50% of all business meals and entertainment costs.

Wouldn't it be nice to deduct the costs of your lavish fine dining and entertainment? Sure it would. While the taxman won't allow a full deduction, the legislation will allow you to deduct 50% of those costs where they were incurred *for the purpose of earning business income*. The key is to make, as far as possible, your nights out on the town business related. So, next time you take in a hockey game, take along a client or potential client.

What We Have Learned:
- *fifty percent of all meals and entertainment costs can be deducted where they were incurred for the purpose of earning business income.*
- *make your nights out on the town business related as far as possible.*

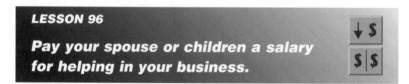

LESSON 96

Pay your spouse or children a salary for helping in your business.

This idea will allow you to have your cake and eat it too. Not only can you reduce your taxable income by claiming a deduction for salary to a spouse or child, but you're keeping the money in the family too. The only requirement is that the salary must be reasonable for the services provided by your family member. Fortunately, Revenue Canada has typically been flexible when interpreting what a reasonable salary is, as long as services are truly being provided.

There's an old court case about a farmer who paid his five year old son to collect eggs every morning. He deducted the cost of his child's services from his income. One conclusion that the judge came to was that a five year old could in fact do productive work and be paid for it – so don't rule out any of your children! The type of work for your spouse or child could include bookkeeping, general office duties, or acting as a director of the company where you operate through a corporation. Consider paying your spouse consulting income rather than a salary. This way, he or she can claim deductions against the income – which could result in a double deduction where your spouse shares the office at home and claims some of those home office expenses against his or her income as well. This last idea is aggressive, so visit your tax professional to talk it over before trying it. This whole idea of paying money to your family is excellent for splitting income (see lesson 32, number 27).

What We Have Learned:
- *paying a salary to your spouse or child will provide a reduction in your taxable income while splitting income at the same time, and will keep the money in the family.*
- *the salary must be reasonable for the services provided.*

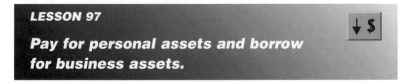

LESSON 97

↓ $

Pay for personal assets and borrow for business assets.

If you're thinking of borrowing money to finance the purchase of a cottage, boat, home entertainment system, a second car, or any other personal asset – think again. You'll be better off if you borrow to buy assets that you're going to use in your business, and pay for personal assets outright. The reason is simple: the interest on the debt will be deductible when you borrow for business purposes. In fact, you should get in the habit of asking yourself one question every time you think of borrowing: *is there a way I can make the interest deductible?* An asset doesn't have to be fully used for business purposes to benefit from an interest deduction. If an asset – a home computer for example – is used partially in the business, then a portion of the interest will be deductible against your business income.

This idea is applicable when you borrow for any reason, not just for the purchase of assets. If you borrow to go on a personal vacation, for example, consider turning the trip into a business trip to make part of the interest deductible. Alternatively, borrow for a legitimate business trip and pay for your personal vacation outright to make interest deductible. Refer back to lesson 10 for more on interest deductibility.

What We Have Learned:
- *where you have the choice, always buy personal assets outright and borrow to buy business assets to make interest deductible.*
- *refer to lesson 10 for more on interest deductibility.*

LESSON 98

↓ $

Apply losses from your business to the most advantageous year.

Revenue Canada has been kind enough to give you a break where you've lost money in a business. First, you'll be required to apply those losses against income from other businesses or sources of income in the current year to the extent possible, but you might still be left with unused losses. Where this happens, you'll be able to apply those losses against income from other years to reduce your taxable income. For regular business losses, called *non-capital losses,* you can carry the losses back three years, or forward seven years to offset taxable income in any of those years. After seven years, the losses expire and can no longer be used. *Capital losses* which arise on the disposition of capital property can only be applied against capital gains, but can be carried back three years or forward indefinitely. Whenever you carry back either non-capital or capital losses, be sure to first apply those losses to the earliest year possible so that you don't lose the opportunity to offset income in those years.

When you have non-capital losses to use up, consider whether you should hold onto the losses and use them in a year when your marginal tax rate is higher.

Karen's Losses

Karen is self-employed. She went into business at the start of 1996 and expects to have a loss of about $10,000 for tax purposes in 1996. If she applies the loss to her taxable income in 1995, she can get back some of the tax she paid. The amount she would recover is $2,700 since her taxable income in 1995 was $29,590 and her marginal tax rate was 27%. Alternatively, Karen could save the loss to apply against her 1997 income. She expects to have taxable income in 1997 of about $60,000, and so a $10,000 loss will save her $5,000 in taxes since her marginal tax rate will be 50%. By waiting until 1997 when her marginal rate is higher, she can save an additional $2,300 ($5,000 − $2,700). If Karen's estimate of income for 1997 is wrong and she can't use the losses in that year, she can always go back and apply the losses to her 1995 taxable income at that future time.

Keep in mind that every Canadian receives his or her first $6,456 of income tax-free due to the basic personal credit available (see lesson 85), so using your losses to bring your taxable income down to $6,456 makes sense (or some higher figure where you have additional non-refundable credits like tuition that must be used in the year), but don't bring your income below this non-taxable level.

One last thing. Where you have losses that are about to expire in a year or two, do all you can to increase your income to a level that will allow you to use them up. This may mean triggering capital gains by selling and repurchasing investments, or reducing discretionary expenses like CCA to increase taxable income, allowing use of your losses.

What We Have Learned:
- *non-capital (business) losses can be carried back three years and forward seven years to shelter taxable income; capital losses can be carried back three years and forward indefinitely, but can only be applied against capital gains.*
- *use non-capital losses in years when you anticipate your marginal tax rate to be higher.*

- *never bring taxable income below $6,456 (or your non-taxable level) when using losses to reduce income.*
- *consider ways to increase taxable income to take advantage of non-capital losses that are about to expire.*

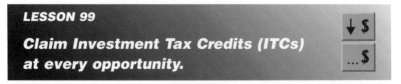

LESSON 99

Claim Investment Tax Credits (ITCs) at every opportunity.

Gary Bateman, our firm's founder, wrote the *Guide to the Taxation of R&D Expenses* published by Carswell. So we'd be remiss if we didn't mention the very generous tax savings that our government offers to individuals, and especially corporations, who invest money in Scientific Research and Experimental Development (SR&ED).

If you're an individual doing R&D you'll be eligible for Investment Tax Credits (ITCs) equal to 20% of the costs you've incurred in the prosecution of R&D. Even better, up to 40% of these ITCs are refundable, meaning the taxman will write you a cheque for up to 40% of those costs, while the remainder of the ITCs can be applied to reduce your taxes payable. ITCs can be carried back three years and forward ten years if not used currently. The ITCs will be taxed in your hands the year after you claim them, but they're still a generous benefit. Corporations receive even more generous ITCs (up to 35% and fully refundable) than individuals, so if you think you're doing R&D you may be wise to incorporate, and you should definitely familiarize yourself with Revenue Canada's form T661, Information Circular 86-4R3, and Interpretation Bulletin 151-R4 as a start. Alternatively, if you have Internet access you can find a summary of these rules, methodology, and forms at our web site: http://www.bateman-mackay.com.

R&D: Who Me?

Most people assume that R&D is only done by large hi-tech corporations who are manufacturers. Nothing could be further from the truth. While we don't have the time or space to do it justice here, we'll try to identify some of the things that will determine whether or not you're doing R&D. If you can answer YES to all of the following questions, you're probably doing R&D:

ARE YOU DOING R&D?

1. Have you or your business ever developed or improved any material, product, process or device by using science or technology to find an answer that was not "readily available" to you otherwise?
2. Was there an element of *technological advancement:* if your devised material, product, process or device had worked (whether it did or not is not the issue) would the findings have added to *your* business's technical knowledge base (not necessarily the knowledge base of society at large)?
3. Was there an element of *technological uncertainty:* in the course of devising the material, product, process, or device, was there uncertainty as to whether or not it would actually work, or was there uncertainty as to the best method to achieve the intended results?
4. Was there *scientific content:* was your testing of the devised material, product, process, or device carried out in an organized fashion, with documentation of results? And, did those supervising the project(s) have relevant training or experience in the field(s) of science or technology involved?

The last three questions introduce the three criteria necessary for R&D. Picture a three-legged stool, and each of these criteria is a leg of the stool. In order to support your R&D claim, all three legs must be present: technological advancement, technological uncertainty, and scientific content. Work in certain areas, including the social sciences and humanities, won't generally qualify as an eligible field of R&D. To qualify for the R&D incentives you must be carrying on business in Canada, and you'll have to file the required forms on time and properly completed. In particular, forms T661 and T2038 with complete documentation are required. Again, calling a tax professional with experience in R&D claims is especially important since all R&D claims are audited by Revenue Canada.

ITCs may also be available to you for expenses other than R&D expenses – for example, where you have invested money, as part of your business, in certain buildings or machinery and equipment. The rules surrounding these ITCs are complex so we recommend that you call a tax professional for help.

What We Have Learned:
- *Investment Tax Credits (ITCs) are generous credits that can reduce your tax bill and provide a cash refund in certain cases where you're doing R&D.*
- *more individuals and companies are doing R&D than realize it.*
- *understand the three-legged stool that constitutes R&D: technological advancement, technological uncertainty, and scientific content.*
- *see a tax professional with experience in filing R&D claims since all claims are audited by Revenue Canada.*
- *Aside from R&D, ITCs may be available for investment in certain buildings, machinery and equipment.*

Structuring Your Business

LESSON 100

Choose the right business structure for your business.

A lot of people assume that operating your own business involves setting up a corporation. Not so. In fact, our discussion so far in this chapter assumes that your business is not incorporated. Carrying on a business is something completely separate from setting up a corporation. There are basically three ways you can run a business: as a proprietor, partnership, or as a corporation.

Proprietorship
A proprietorship is not a separate legal entity. It's just you running a business under whatever name you choose. For example, your child who sets up a lemonade stand at the end of the driveway and puts up a sign "Lisa's Lemonade" is actually operating a proprietorship (the only difference between you and your child is that you hope to make more money and to reduce your tax bill). There's no legal distinction between you and the business, so you won't be able to pay yourself a salary; any money you take out of the business is a draw, and is not taxable. You'll pay tax personally on profits earned by the business, and you'll be able to apply losses from the business against your other personal income. Finally, you'll be liable personally for all debts of the business.

Partnership

A partnership is legally defined as the relationship that exists between persons carrying on a business in common with a view to profit. It's much like two or more proprietors getting together to run one common business. The partnership calculates the profit or loss of the business and then allocates that profit or loss to each of the partners who pay tax on any income on their personal tax returns. In this way, the partnership itself doesn't pay tax, although information returns (not tax returns) are required to be filed. Like a proprietorship, a partnership cannot pay the partners a salary, rather the money taken out is a non-taxable draw. Each partner will pay tax on his or her allocation of the partnership's profits. In most partnerships, the partners are jointly and severally liable for the debts of the business (unless it's a limited partnership in which the partner is not actively involved).

Corporation

A corporation is a separate legal entity. In fact, when the Income Tax Act refers to a *person,* it could be referring to a corporation, among other things. A corporation is required to file its own tax returns and to maintain a more detailed set of accounting records. As a result, there are usually some ongoing costs involved in maintaining a corporation such as financial statement preparation, federal and provincial tax return preparation, and bookkeeping costs, in addition to the initial costs to set up the corporation.

Generally, you *should not* set up a corporation for your business until the business has grown in size and profitability. The main reason for this is complexity – and this complexity is reflected in the higher costs of maintaining a corporation. A second reason is that, where you're a proprietor and you incur losses in your first few years in business, these losses can be applied to reduce your other personal income or to recover personal taxes that you've paid in the last three years. If you were to incorporate at the outset of your business and incurred losses in the first few years, those losses would be trapped in the corporation and would be available to offset profits of the corporation only – and if there were no profits in the next seven years, the losses would expire. A corporation does offer limited liability since the shareholders are not liable for the debts of the company, although a director of the corporation (you) would be liable for certain debts in many situations.

What We Have Learned:
- *there are three ways you can run your business: as a proprietorship, partnership, or a corporation.*
- *unlike the others, a corporation is a separate legal entity and will offer limited liability to shareholders.*
- *setting up a corporation is not advisable until the business has grown in size and profitability.*

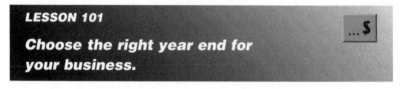

LESSON 101

Choose the right year end for your business.

If you're a proprietor or partner you have the option of choosing any date in the year as your business's year end. There used to be great advantages to choosing a year end in January – this is how it worked: you could defer taxes for one full year by choosing a January 31st year end. For example, if your unincorporated business earned $40,000 for the year ended January 31, 1994, you were not required to include the $40,000 in your personal income until you filed your 1994 tax return on April 30, 1995 – a full one year deferral. Unfortunately, changes made in the February 1995 federal budget significantly reduced the benefits of doing this.

In a nutshell, here's how the new rules work: if you're a proprietor or partner your tax return will be filed for the calendar year. If your business year (called your *fiscal* year) does not end on December 31st, you'll have to adjust your business's income to reflect a December 31st year end. How? If, for example, your fiscal year ends on September 30, 1997 you'll have to calculate the business's income for the twelve months ending on September 30, 1997 and then arbitrarily add 3/12ths of that number to convert your income to a December 31, 1997 year end. You'll also subtract 3/12ths of your 1996 income so that the total income you're reporting is for a twelve month period, and not a fifteen month period.

You do have the option at any time of moving your proprietorship's or partnership's fiscal year end to December 31st to simplify your tax calculations. In many cases it may be worth your while to do this. Where you're incurring losses, a December 31st year end will be to your advantage since you can apply those losses against other sources of income sooner than you would otherwise. Although the opportunity is not what it used to be, you might still be able to defer taxes by maintaining a year end other than December 31st if your business has been operating for at least a year (refer to lesson 35, point 19 for more details). If you're just starting a business this year you probably won't want to choose a non-calendar year end since, going back to our example above, you would add 3/12ths to your income, but you wouldn't get an offsetting 3/12ths deduction for the prior year's income. Visit a tax professional to make an informed decision as to the best year end date for your business.

The year end of a corporation can be any date you'd like. By the way, once you've chosen a year end for your corporation, you cannot arbitrarily change it in a subsequent year. Revenue Canada has to approve a change in year end, and you'll have to convince them that there are good business reasons (not tax reasons) for wanting a change.

Since a corporation will file its own tax returns within six months of its year end anyway, there's no single attractive time of the year to set a corporate year end. Two things to consider will be: (1) your business cycle, and (2) whether your accountant will give you a break on your fees if you choose a year end that will keep him or her busy in the summer months. Regarding your business cycle, it would be wise to choose a year end that falls when things are typically slow. A landscaping company, for example, may choose a December 31st year end since there's more time to deal with accounting and tax issues when there's less other work to do. There may be one situation where your corporation should have a specific year end: when it's a foreign corporation designed to defer income (see lesson 35, point 24).

What We Have Learned:
- *proprietorships and partnerships can choose any year end desired, however a December 31st year end may make the most sense given new rules introduced in the February 1995 federal budget, especially for new businesses in their first year.*
- *corporations can choose whatever year end is desired.*
- *refer to lesson 35 for more information.*

Payments To The Taxman

LESSON 102

Save $1,150 in Unemployment Insurance premiums when self-employed.

One of the benefits to being self-employed is that you're not required to pay Unemployment Insurance (UI) premiums. This will save you over $1,150 in 1996 (over $2,760 when taking into account both the employee and employer portions). The flip side of this is that you won't be eligible to collect UI if you ever decided to try. This is, to some people, enough to convince them that self-employment is a bad idea. Here's an interesting fact: if it's not entirely clear whether you're an employee or a consultant, Revenue Canada may look to see whether or not you tried to collect UI when your "consulting" contract was over. If you did try to collect, this fact could be used against you as an argument that you were in fact an employee – so be careful.

What We Have Learned:
- *if you're self-employed, you're not required to pay UI premiums, which will save you about $1,150 in 1996.*
- *you won't be eligible to claim UI if you're self-employed.*
- *trying to claim UI after a "consulting" contract ends could convince the taxman that you were actually an employee and not a consultant.*

LESSON 103

Plan for Canada Pension Plan contributions when self-employed.

Unlike UI premiums, when you're self-employed you'll be required to make contributions to the Canada Pension Plan when you file your tax return in April. Employees have one half of this tab picked up by their employers who match contributions made by their employees. Where you're self-employed, however, you'll have to pick up both the employer and employee portion. In 1996 this could amount to a maximum of about $1,786 which you'll reach when your self-employment income is $35,400 or more (the calculation is 5.6% of income over $3,500 until the maximum $1,786 is reached). This tax hit will be partially offset by a tax credit available on your tax return for the CPP contributions paid. The credit will be worth about 27% of your premiums, depending on your province, so the credit will be about $480 when you're paying the maximum $1,786 in contributions. In this case, your actual cost of CPP contributions will be $1,306 ($1,786-$480).

You'll need to make your CPP payments in quarterly instalments as part of your income tax instalments if you're required to make these (see lesson 105). These CPP contributions are due to increase each year in accordance with a federal-provincial agreement dating back to 1985. The contributions will move from their current 5.6% to 8.6% in 2011 at which time you'll be paying about $1,000 more each year in CPP contributions than you are today. And from the way things appear, we'd bet that the increases due to come will be even higher than they are currently budgeted to be. All of this means that it's even more important that you minimize your income taxes – to offset the unavoidable increase in future CPP contributions.

What We Have Learned:
- *if you're self-employed you'll be required to make CPP contributions which could amount to a maximum of about $1,786 in 1996.*
- *you'll get some of those premiums back in the form of a credit equal to 27% of the premiums paid.*
- *CPP contributions are due to increase significantly over the coming years – all the more reason to minimize your income taxes.*

LESSON 104

Plan for provincial payroll taxes when self-employed.

Provincial payroll taxes were "invented" in Manitoba and have spread across the country as another disincentive to hiring employees. Depending on your province, you might be subject to provincial payroll taxes on your self-employment income since some provinces have extended these taxes to the self-employed. For example, in Ontario, an Employer Health Tax (EHT) will apply where your net income from self-employment is more than $40,000. The amount of the tax will be about 0.76% of your income between $40,000 and $200,000. Once your income is over $200,000 the rate increases gradually until you hit the top rate of about 1.52% of net income. Employers are permitted a deduction for Ontario EHT paid for employees, although you won't be allowed a deduction when you're self-employed. To compensate, you will, in effect, pay a lower rate than employers are required to pay for their employees.

What We Have Learned:
• *where you're self-employed, watch for provincial payroll taxes that you may be required to pay, like Ontario's EHT.*

LESSON 105
Consider whether tax instalments might be necessary.

This lesson can apply not only to the self-employed, but to retirees as well, since both often receive income without tax deducted at the source. Unlike employees whose earnings are subject to tax being deducted at the source, self-employed taxpayers are responsible for remitting their own tax payments. Unfortunately, Revenue Canada won't allow you to wait until April 30th each year to send them your full taxes owing for the previous calendar year. The government insists that you make tax instalments throughout the year to cover the liability for that year. There are some exceptions to the instalment requirement.

Instalments: Do You Have To Pay Them?
New rules were introduced effective July 1, 1994 regarding instalments. Generally, where you regularly owe Revenue Canada more than $2,000 in April ($1,200 in Quebec) you'll be required to make instalments. Specifically, if your tax balance owing exceeded $2,000 in either of the two preceding years, and you expect the same result for the current year, you're required to make instalments for the cur-

rent year on March 15th, June 15th, September 15th, and December 15th.

Donna's Instalments

Donna is employed, but earns quite a bit of part-time business income each year that is not subject to tax withheld at the source. For her 1994 tax year, Donna had to cut a cheque to Revenue Canada for $1,100 in April to cover her taxes on the extra income. The next year, she had to write a cheque for $2,200 to Revenue Canada for the same reason. For 1996, she expects that she'll have income similar to 1995, so she'll probably have to write a cheque for about $2,200 again. Donna is required to make instalments for 1996 because her total balance owing for 1996 is expected to be over $2,000 ($1,200 in Quebec) and she owed over $2,000 in one of the two preceding years (1995 she owed over $2,000 when she filed her return). If Donna's business takes a turn for the worse, and she expects her income for 1996 to be lower, so that she won't be required to remit over $2,000 when filing her 1996 tax return, she'll escape the requirement to pay instalments. If she's wrong though, the taxman will ask for interest and penalties on the instalments that should have been made.

The threshold is lower in Quebec since the federal government does not collect tax for that province, and so the provincial portion of the tax is excluded in the threshold amount. To determine whether you'll have to make instalments, you'll need to calculate your tax balance owing for the previous two years, and estimate the balance owing for the current year. The tax balance owing is calculated as your total taxes payable on line 435 of your return, less all the credits on lines 437 through 479 except the instalment credit on line 476.

How Much Should The Instalments Be?

Once you've determined that instalments are required, you'll have to determine how much those instalments should be. There are two ways to do this.

1. INSTALMENT NOTICES. If your tax balance owing for any year is over $2,000, Revenue Canada will send you instalment reminders for the following year. These reminders will come two-at-a-time. For example, in February you should receive notices for your March 15th and June 15th instalments, and in August you'll receive notices for September 15th and December 15th. These instalment amounts

calculated by Revenue Canada are based on your tax liabilities for the previous two years. Where you expect your income to decline in the current year, consider the option of calculating the instalments yourself.

2. CALCULATING YOUR OWN INSTALMENTS. You're allowed to make your own instalment calculations if you want. You should use form T1033-WS for this purpose. There are three permissible ways of making the calculation, as follows: (1) the same way Revenue Canada makes the calculation for the notices, (2) based only on the prior year tax liability, and (3) based on the current year expected tax liability. If you use option 3 and remit deficient instalments, you could face interest and penalties, so beware.

What We Have Learned:

- *where you have income that's not subject to tax withheld at the source, you may be required to make quarterly instalments where your expected tax balance owing for the current year and the actual balance for either of the two preceding years is over $2,000 ($1,200 in Quebec).*

- *there are two ways to determine the amount of your instalments: let Revenue Canada do the calculations, or calculate them yourself.*

- *calculate them yourself when you expect your income to be lower this year than last year since this will minimize your instalments.*

Part III

Investing Your Money

Investment Basics

9

Investing your money can often be a stressful and bewildering process, however it's the belief of many professional money managers that it doesn't have to be – if some simple concepts are understood and some straightforward principles followed. This chapter is intended to introduce these principles to you.

Risk and Return

The first principle is that there's a relationship between risk and return. Generally, the rate of return on any investment varies directly with the degree of risk involved. That is, the higher the risk, the higher the promised rate of return. It would be nice, for example, to achieve an annual rate of return of 20% on your low-risk GICs, but it's not going to happen. Invest in the stock of a risky hi-tech company and you could find the 20% or more that you're looking for. Of course, unlike GICs, the hi-tech stock brings with it the possibility that you could lose part or all of your original investment. The old saying *you can't get something for nothing* is true in the world of investments. It's obvious from our GIC versus hi-tech stock example that different types of investments carry different levels of risk, and in fact, different *types* of risk. Before talking about these risks, let's talk about the different *classes* of investments.

LESSON 106

Understand the 3 different investment classes.

Any investment you buy will fit into one of three classes: money market investments, fixed-income investments, or equity investments.

Money Market Investments

Money market investments are the least risky and, as a result, usually offer lower returns than other investments. These investments are basically short-term cash and cash-equivalent types of investments that include bank accounts, treasury bills, Canada Savings Bonds, term deposits, and GICs among other things. A characteristic of money market investments is that they are low-risk (often because they are government-guaranteed), but are highly taxed since they generally pay interest income only. These investments aren't completely risk-free either; they're subject to certain types of risks which we'll look at in a minute.

Fixed-Income Investments

Fixed-income investments are a little more risky than money market investments, and therefore usually offer a slightly higher return. Again, we'll be looking at the types of risks momentarily. As the name implies, these investments generally provide a fixed rate of income over the life of the investment. These include, for example, bonds, debentures, preferred shares, and mortgages. Fixed-income investments generally pay interest income (although preferred shares offer dividends), and they usually offer capital gains in an environment where interest rates are falling, although predicting the direction of interest rate moves is difficult. The interest income is highly taxed, but the dividends and capital gains, if any, are taxed more favourably, so these investments can offer a higher after-tax rate of return than money market investments.

Equity Investments

Maybe you've heard the phrase *be an owner not a loaner.* When you invest in equities, this is precisely what you're doing. Money market and fixed-income investments make you a loaner – that is, you're lending your money to someone else in return for interest on your capital. Equities make you an owner, and wherever there's ownership, there's more risk involved (what you own could drop in value). Equities include ownership in assets like common shares, warrants, and rights, or direct ownership in tangible assets like real estate, gold, and similar investments. These investments provide for potential capital gains, and dividend income in the case of shares in a company, both of which are taxed at lower marginal rates than interest income – see lesson 36.

What We Have Learned:
- *there are three different classes of investments: money market, fixed-income, and equity investments.*
- *each class offers a different level of risk with money market being the least risky, fixed-income in the middle, and equities being most risky.*
- *lower risk offers a lower return and higher taxes.*
- *higher risk offers a higher return and lower taxes.*

LESSON 107
Understand the different types of risk.

Each class of investment carries different *types* of risk. As we mentioned, even lower-risk investments (like money market securities) are subject to certain kinds of risk. You need to decide what types of risk you're willing to live with, and we'll give some help with this in lesson 108, but first, let's look at the main risk types to consider when building your portfolio.

Inflation or purchasing power risk
This is the risk that the return on your investments won't keep pace with the rate of inflation. For example, if you earn 8% on a GIC and pay 50% of that in taxes, your after-tax return is just 4%. But did you really earn 4%? Not after inflation. If inflation was 5% for the year, you've actually lost 1% of purchasing power. In other words, your *real rate of return* was negative 1%. Generally, money market and fixed-income investments are victims of this kind of risk. Equities are more likely to provide protection here.

Liquidity risk

This is the risk that you won't be able to convert your investment into cash when you need to. You'll find that equity investments are victims to this risk while fixed-income and, to a greater extent, money market investments offer protection against liquidity risk.

Market risk

There are two parts to market risk: *class risk* (the risk that a general class or industry that you've invested in goes down on the whole), and *business risk* (the risk that a particular stock, real estate, or other specific investment has a poor return on its own). Equity investments, and to some extent fixed-income investments, are the victims of this risk. Money market investments will generally protect you from market risk.

These three types of risk are all-encompassing. Additional names for risk such as *currency rate risk* (when investing in foreign countries) and *interest rate risk* (when investing in long-term debt instruments) are, in our opinion, really subsets of the three types mentioned above: inflation, liquidity and market risk.

What We Have Learned:

- *there are 3 categories of risk when investing: inflation risk, liquidity risk, and market risk.*
- *you'll need to decide which risks are of most concern to you and what your tolerance of each risk will be.*

LESSON 108

Know how to determine your risk tolerances.

Your tolerance for the different types of risk will always be based on your specific objectives and circumstances. In particular, your age, income level, and debt load should play an important role in determining how much risk you're willing to take on. For example, a young professional in his or her early thirties with no debt, high income and no dependents will probably worry less about *market risk* (the risk of fluctuations in value) than a seventy year old on a fixed pension, because the younger person knows that there is plenty of time to recover from downward fluctuations in any investments before retirement.

Likewise, the same seventy year old will probably shy away from *liquidity risk* (the risk that you won't be able to cash-in investments on a timely basis) because of the need to draw on investments to meet daily living expenses. If the money is tied up in an investment that offers poor liquidity (real estate for example), it may be difficult to sell the investment quickly enough to provide the income needed for daily living.

Similarly, our elderly friend may decide that, although there is the need to protect purchasing power since he or she is on a fixed-income, some *inflation risk* (the risk that you'll lose purchasing power) will have to be tolerated in order to preserve capital and avoid the market risk attached to certain equity investments.

Keep in mind that you can usually put together an investment portfolio that will satisfy your objectives and offer just the right balance of these risks for your taste and circumstances. Experienced financial planners can ask you questions to help determine an appropriate portfolio, but the basic question becomes: *what am I willing to risk for the return I want to receive?*

What We Have Learned:

- *deciding which risks to tolerate and which to avoid will depend on your specific objectives and circumstances, particularly your perception of these risks keeping in mind your age, income level, and debt load.*
- *an experienced financial planner can assist in setting objectives, assessing risk tolerance, and determining an appropriate portfolio, but the basic question becomes: what am I willing to risk for the return I want to receive?*

How To Invest

Now let's talk about *how* to invest your money. We'll talk about *where* specifically to put your money in the next chapter. For now, let's focus on questions like:

- How do I choose specific investments?
- How do I minimize my risks?
- Who should invest for me?

LESSON 109

Choose strategic investment by class allocation over market timing.

Many people play the stock market based on "tips" of the next big score. They try to choose their investments based on high, short-term paybacks. This is called *market timing,* or *speculation,* and to make money this way you need a strong heart and lots of luck. *Strategic investment* is something different altogether – it focuses on the long-term allocation of your money to achieve your objectives within acceptable risk levels.

Research studies[3] have shown that approximately 80 to 90% of your portfolio's rate of return is determined by the *class allocation* (the split between money market, fixed-income, and equities) rather than the allocation of your money to *specific investments.* In other words, you'll earn your money on the basis of your long-term asset mix by class (money market, fixed-income, and equities) as opposed to the specific stocks, bonds, and other securities purchased within each class, or from trying to time the market for peaks and troughs. Strategic investment by class allocation is, therefore, the way to go.

Putting Theory Into Practice

So now it's time to invest and you're wondering how to take our *strategic investment by class allocation* principle and put it into practice. There are three steps to doing this.

1. ALLOCATE TO INVESTMENT CLASSES. The first step is to decide what percentage of your money will be invested in each of the three investment classes: money market, fixed-income, and equities. How do you do this? Start with a generally accepted rule of thumb: the percentage in equities should be equal to 100 minus your age. A 40 year old, for example, should have about 60% (100-40) of his or her money in equities. This percentage should be tailored for your risk tolerance. For example, if you're a 40 year old who likes to avoid risk at all cost, you'll want to reduce the 60% rule of thumb to perhaps 40%. Once you've decided how much to put into equities, allocate

---

[3]   In particular, "Determinants of portfolio performance," The Financial Analysts Journal, 1986, authors Brinson, Hood and Beebower.

the remainder to fixed-income and money market investments based on your liquidity needs. Our 40 year old friend, for example, may not be relying on his or her investments to provide cash on short notice, and so perhaps only 5% will be invested in money market investments while the remainder will be invested in fixed-income securities.

2. CHOOSE SPECIFIC SECURITIES. Once you've allocated your money to the three classes, you're in a position to decide on specific investments within each class. Our 40 year old friend, for example, may invest his or her 60% allocated to equities in any number of equity investments: equity mutual funds, common shares, real estate, among other investments. The 5% allocated to money market investments could be put into treasury bills, term deposits, or a bank account, among other things. The final 35% allocated to fixed income could be split between corporate bonds, preferred shares, mortgages, or other similar investments. You may want to consult an investment broker to determine the specific mutual funds, shares, bonds, or other investments to invest in.

3. RE-EVALUATE YOUR ALLOCATION PERIODICALLY. Once you've made an allocation to the three classes, and you've chosen specific investments, you should monitor your portfolio at least once each year, and ideally every six months. Since you're investing for the long-term and not trying to time the market it's not necessary to review your investments on a daily basis. When you re-evaluate your allocation, look at both your class allocation and the specific investments chosen. You may want to trust this monitoring process to a good investment broker who may have the time and expertise to watch over your portfolio, but remember, the investments are still yours and you should keep an eye on them. Your broker should provide you with reports on a regular basis that can help you to keep watch over things, although the reports are not always ideal for this purpose.

What We Have Learned:
- *avoid trying to time the market to maximize your investment returns; invest for the long-term instead.*
- *most of your investment returns will come from the class allocation of your money, not from allocation to specific investments.*

- *allocate your money, according to your objectives and risk toler-ances, to investment classes first, then choose specific securities within each class.*

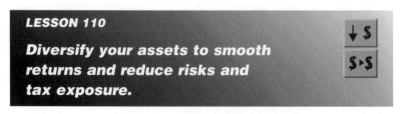

LESSON 110

Diversify your assets to smooth returns and reduce risks and tax exposure.

You've heard them say *don't put all your eggs in one basket.* The person who came up with these wise words must have worked in the invest-ment industry. Apparently he followed up the achievement by coin-ing the term *diversification* to more succinctly express the principle. By diversifying you can minimize your exposure to the different types of risk.

You see, the three investment classes do not generally move in tandem. In a year where fixed-income or money-market investments offer a decent rate of return, equities may offer dismal returns, and visa versa. For example, in 1980 long-term bonds (fixed-income) offered a rate of return of just 2.1% while 91-day treasury bills (money-market) offered 15%, and the TSE 300 (equities) offered a return of 30.1%. In 1991 those same bonds offered a 25% return while treasury bills offered 9.8%, and the TSE 300 provided a return of 12%.

Canadian equity markets tend to move in the opposite direction of Canadian bond markets. Why? It's simply that when interest rates are lower, investors tend to move out of bonds and into equities since lower interest rates mean lower coupon rates offered by bonds but increased business activity and profits for companies. Conversely, when interest rates are high, investors move back into bonds since bonds offer an attractive yield while the higher rates slow down economic activity and shrink corporate profits, making equities less attractive. This relationship isn't always true – equity and bond markets don't always move in opposite directions, but as a general rule, they do.

By investing in more than one class, and in more than one specif-ic investment within each class, you'll be able to smooth out the ups and downs that each class will go through individually. The result is that the overall rate of return on your investment portfolio will be more consistent from year to year, and not subject to the same level of fluctuation that you'd experience if you had your money invested completely in one class.

Experience has shown that, while you may reduce slightly the overall return of your portfolio by diversifying, your risk drops significantly. For example, investing fully in equities might provide, say, a 13% rate of return over a 10 year period, but your level of risk will be very high (you could've just as easily had a 5% return over that period). By diversifying properly you might reduce the overall rate of your portfolio to, say, 12% over that same period, but your risk will have dropped significantly – the 12% was more of a "sure thing" (although nothing is for sure) than the 13% was.

Lastly, the marginal tax rates on certain investment classes (money market and fixed-income) are higher than others (equities) and by diversifying you'll not only reduce your risks, but reduce your tax exposure as well.

What We Have Learned:
- *different investment classes do not move in tandem.*
- *diversify by not putting all your eggs in one basket.*
- *diversifying will make investment returns more consistent from year to year while reducing your risk and tax exposure.*

LESSON 111
Don't forget to diversify internationally.

We've talked about the importance of investing outside of Canada in lesson 78. It's apparent that when some countries are in deep recessions others are experiencing economic growth. The gloomy term *world-wide recession* periodically used by the media is really a fallacy: where investment opportunities are poor at home, there are always opportunities somewhere else. Refer back to lesson 78 for specifics on the three good reasons to hold foreign content in your portfolio. Specifically, foreign content will: maximize returns, expand selection, and reduce exposure to volatile or stagnant markets.

What We Have Learned:
- *diversify by holding foreign content inside your investment port-folio.*
- *refer to lesson 78 for details on the three benefits of foreign content.*

LESSON 112

Understand and select your own investments.

Peter Lynch, retired manager of the world's largest mutual fund (Fidelity Magellan), had achieved an average annual return of more than 30% during the 13 years of his management. During a 1992 speech he was quoted as saying that, "the average individual has been convinced by the media that they don't stand a chance against the pros with their computers and degrees. That is wrong, dead wrong!"

In his view, the average person often has the opportunity to see things months or years before professional investors. An example: "...how many doctors have ever told you to buy stock in a pharmaceutical company?...but all kinds will talk about the latest tip on a mining venture or oil stock (that a pro told them about)." Lynch is a firm believer that you should invest in what you understand. One thing that Lynch's wife understood very well was pantyhose. One day she came home from the grocery store with three plastic eggs filled with pantyhose. She was so impressed with the L'eggs display at the store, that Lynch took notice. His wife insisted that women loved the marketing idea, and that these L'eggs were disappearing from the rack faster than they could be re-stocked. So he bought shares in Hanes, the company who manufactures L'eggs, and the stock turned out to be an excellent performer for his Fidelity Magellan mutual fund. The rule of thumb is simple: invest in what you understand, and if you don't understand it, keep away from it.

Still skeptical that you have what it takes to make smart investment decisions? Lynch further commented on a survey that showed that of the 8,000 investment clubs in the U.S. in which club members (rather than investment professionals) pick the investments,

60% outperform the market averages. Only 25% of professional investors tend to beat these averages.

If you're not comfortable with the idea of selecting your own investments, consider help from an investment broker. You'd be wise to remember that he's dealing with your money, so it's still your responsibility to make sure he's only investing in things you understand. Let him make recommendations for you, but you should make the final decision on every investment so that *you* are selecting where your money goes.

What We Have Learned:
- *you don't have to be a professional investor to make good investment decisions on your own – just look for investments that you understand.*
- *obtain recommendations from an investment broker if you want, but understand each investment, and make the final decision about each investment on your own.*

Your Investment Advisor

LESSON 113

Learn how to choose the right investment advisor.

There are a number of people out there who are qualified to help you with your investment decisions. Generally, your C.A. will not advise on specific securities to invest in, although he or she may be able to help you identify your objectives and assess your tolerance for risk. For help in choosing specific securities, you'll do well to approach either a Registered Financial Planner (RFP) or an investment broker with an appropriate level of education and experience. Choose someone who you feel comfortable speaking with, and we'd recommend an investment broker who has, as a minimum, a university degree, and preferably one who has a C.A. designation or an MBA. You'll find these investment brokers in all of the major brokerage houses, and your C.A. could certainly recommend someone to you.

You should understand what your advisor is supposed to be doing for you and how he or she is being paid. Financial planners and brokers are paid commissions for selling certain investments to you. These commissions can range from 2% for discount brokers, to a 3% or 4% standard fee for most mutual funds, and up to 8 or 9% for some limited partnerships. You should be aware that many mutual funds and investments are sold directly by fund companies and banks for no load or commission.

Be aware that it's in the best interest of an investment broker to sell you investments that are going to yield the highest commissions. It's generally wise to ask any investment professional what his or her commission is on any investment. If you can't get a straight answer, it's probably very high. This doesn't mean you should avoid the investment, it just means you should carefully assess for yourself whether the investment is appropriate for your objectives and risk tolerance. Where the commissions to your broker are high, you should ask what criteria was used when he or she recommended the investment, and how it fits in with your objectives and tolerance for risk.

What We Have Learned:
- *choose an investment advisor with an appropriate level of education and experience: an RFP or investment broker with a C.A. designation or an MBA is preferred.*
- *choose someone who you enjoy speaking with.*
- *understand what commissions are being paid to your advisor, and where the commissions are high, determine whether the investment fits in with your objectives and tolerance for risk.*

LESSON 114

Understand that investment brokers and financial planners are generally not tax experts.

Did you hear about the bride who hired a jack-of-all-trades for her wedding? The guy was a limo driver, photographer, and musician all in one. He offered his services at a very good price. As a driver he was quite good (rated 9 out of 10). As a photographer he was so-so (he took as many pictures of his thumb as he did of the bride and groom – 6 out of 10), and as a musician, well, he was advised not to give up his day job (he was a lawyer by day) – 3 out of 10.

There is seldom any single professional who can handle all your needs his or herself, and certainly complex tax issues should be handled by a tax professional who has completed the CICA's In-Depth Tax Course (refer to lesson 7). It's been our experience that the most successful professionals in the financial planning field tend to make use of a variety of specialists while relying on the basic investment principles outlined in this chapter. Be sure to understand what abilities each of your advisors has – this will enable you to build a successful financial planning team.

Take a look at the following table which outlines the general functions of different professionals as far as your investments are concerned.

INVESTMENT PLANNING: THE ROLE OF PROFESSIONALS

DEPTH OF ANALYSIS		
HI	Tax accountants Tax lawyers	Tax accountants with financial planning background Combination of others
		Investment brokers
LO	Discount brokers Insurance agents Banks	Financial planners without in-depth tax training

LO   **BREADTH OF ANALYSIS**   HI

What We Have Learned:
- *there is seldom any single advisor who can meet all your financial planning needs; complex tax advice should be obtained from a tax professional alone (refer to lesson 7).*
- *understand the abilities of each of your advisors so that a successful financial planning team can be put in place.*

LESSON 115

Be sure to minimize your commissions or brokerage fees.

Full service brokers and planners may provide you with needed advice, or alternatives that you may not have been aware of. Where you don't feel comfortable going it alone, a full service broker may be for you. You'll pay more in commissions, but the advice may be worth it, and if you've got a decent sum of money, the commissions are negotiable. Some investors, however, feel confident enough to pick their own investments without advice. An alternative for you is a discount broker. Each of the major banks offers a discount brokerage service where you'll be able to buy and sell securities, but you won't get any help or advice – employees at a discount brokerage are generally not qualified to provide any advice. Commissions charged by discount brokers are generally 1/2% to 2% less than what you'll pay a full services broker.

In any event, you should be aware that many large public companies offer dividend re-investment plans (DRIPs) to shareholders where they can directly invest in additional stock without paying any commissions (see more in lesson 120).

What We Have Learned:

• *minimize your commissions by negotiating with your full service broker or opening a discount brokerage account, and take advantage of DRIPs (see lesson 120).*

Where To Put Your Money

10

Clients often ask us where they should invest their money. Since we're not investment brokers, we don't generally make recommendations on *specific* securities, although we do make recommendations regarding different *types* of securities that are consistent with minimizing taxes and with a client's overall financial objectives.

The ideas that follow are recommended because they will increase your investment returns by minimizing your taxes on the investment income. An exception is lesson 120 which will increase returns, not by minimizing taxes, but by reducing the commissions you pay on the investments.

Before jumping into any of these types of investments, we recommend that you speak to an investment broker about the specific securities available, and about the potential drawbacks.

LESSON 116

Invest in mutual funds, but postpone the purchase until after year end.

Mutual funds are an ideal investment for virtually everyone. They work this way: thousands of small investors like you pool their money together into one fund. The fund is then invested in different types of securities: stocks, bonds, money market instruments, real estate, gold, and the list goes on. Different mutual funds will invest in different types of securities, so you'll need to decide which securities meet your needs best (see lesson 106), and then pick the right mutual fund – and there are well over a thousand to choose from. The main advantages to a mutual fund include: access to professional money management, automatic diversification, and liquidity. When you're investing inside your RRSP, taxes are not a concern, but where you hold your mutual funds outside an RRSP, certain mutual funds may offer more tax relief than others, and we've talked about this in lessons 36 and 37.

We recommend that where you invest in mutual funds outside your RRSP and wait until the last few months of the year to make a purchase, consider holding off on the purchase until January of the following year.

Jim Pays Someone Else's Taxes
Jim had $10,000 to invest and decided, in December 1996, to buy units in ABC mutual fund. So, on December 15, 1996 he bought 1,000 units in the fund at a cost of $10 each. The cost of each unit in ABC fund was $10 throughout the entire month of December. On December 31, 1996, ABC mutual fund paid all its unitholders, including Jim, a distribution of profits of $1 per unit that the fund had realized during 1996. This distribution of income reduced the value of each unit in the fund to $9, but each unitholder, including Jim, received additional units in ABC fund since the $1 distribution was reinvested in more units of the fund. So, at December 31, 1996, Jim now owned units of ABC mutual fund worth $9 each, but he owned 1,111.11 units now instead of the 1,000 units he originally bought since the $1,000 distribution ($1 per unit x 1,000 units) received by Jim was reinvested in 111.11 units ($1,000/$9 per unit) of the fund. Jim's total investment in ABC fund after the distribution was still $10,000 ($9 per unit x 1,111.11 units). So Jim is no worse off after the distribution right? Not quite. The $1,000 distribution received by Jim is taxable to him, and he received a T3 slip reporting the $1,000 distribution. At a marginal tax rate of 50%, this $1,000 distribution cost Jim $500 in taxes. Maybe Jim wouldn't mind paying tax on profits he earned, except that he didn't earn these profits. The $1,000 distribution resulted from profits made by the mutual fund throughout 1996, long before Jim was invested in the fund.

In effect, when you buy into a mutual fund at the end of a year, you'll pay tax on profits that should really be taxed in someone else's hands

– in the hands of those unitholders who had been in the fund all year long. Does this mean you should never buy units in a mutual fund in the last couple months of the year? Not necessarily. If you expect the mutual fund to increase in value between your purchase date and December 31st, perhaps the tax you'll pay on the distribution you receive will be more than offset by an increase in the unit value of the fund.

Whether this happens or not will depend on the length of time until year end, and on the general direction of the securities in the mutual fund. Before buying a fund, speak with an investment broker about whether you're likely to recover the tax cost before December 31st. If you're not sure, wait until January to make a purchase.

Joni Waits Until January

Like Jim, Joni had $10,000 to invest, and wanted to put her money in ABC mutual fund as well. Joni waited until January 1, 1997 to buy her units. The units cost $9 each (refer back to Jim's story) and so she was able to purchase 1,111.11 units in the fund ($10,000/$9). After the purchase, she had 1,111.11 units worth a total of $10,000, which puts her in the same position as Jim on January 1, 1997. The only difference is, Joni didn't have to come up with $500 to pay the tax on somebody else's profits as Jim did.

After buying units in any mutual fund you'll need to monitor its performance on a regular basis. This can be done with the help of a good investment broker, although you can certainly keep track of your fund's performance by reading the financial papers and the business section of the bigger newspapers. See lesson 18 for advice on minimizing your taxes on the disposition of your mutual funds.

What We Have Learned:

- *mutual funds are excellent investments for most investors because they offer professional money management, automatic diversification, and liquidity.*
- *where you invest in mutual funds outside your RRSP and are making a purchase later in the year, consider waiting until January of the following year to avoid paying tax on someone else's gains.*
- *monitor your mutual fund's performance on a regular basis; see lesson 18 for further advice on minimizing taxes on your mutual fund dispositions.*

LESSON 117

Keep at least 1 unit of any mutual fund with an exempt capital gains balance.

If you owned any mutual funds on February 22, 1994 you may have elected to trigger a capital gain when you filed your 1994 tax return in order to take advantage of your capital gains exemption. If you made this election on your 1994 return you would've created an *exempt capital gains balance* for each mutual fund (or other flow-through investment). This exempt balance can be used up until the year 2004 to offset any capital gains arising from the sale of the particular mutual fund or from gains passed along to you by the fund. After 2004, if you have not yet used up the exempt balance, the balance is added to your cost of the investment which will reduce any capital gain or increase a capital loss when you sell your units in the fund.

The exempt capital gains balance is a valuable resource since it will save you tax dollars later if your fund does well enough to make you some money. Unfortunately, if you dispose of all your units in a particular mutual fund that has an exempt balance, you'll lose that balance forever. To avoid this problem, be sure to keep at least one unit in any mutual fund that has an exempt capital gains balance so that, should you decide to buy more of that mutual fund later, you'll still have available the exempt capital gains balance and the opportunity to shelter capital gains from tax.

What We Have Learned:

* *when you filed your 1994 tax return you may have elected to use your capital gains exemption to shelter gains on your mutual funds. If so, you have an exempt capital gains balance available for each mutual fund for which an election was made.*
* *keep at least one unit in each of these mutual funds to protect the right to use this exempt capital gains balance to shelter capital gains in the future.*

LESSON 118

Invest in a mutual fund limited partnership to reduce taxable income.

There are a number of different limited partnerships (LPs) out there competing for the money of investors determined to reduce their taxes. Before talking about mutual fund limited partnerships, let's take a look at what a limited partnership is, how it's supposed to save you tax dollars, and what type of LPs are available out there.

This Thing Called a Limited Partnership

We talked about partnerships in lesson 100. We mentioned that partners are typically liable jointly and severally for the debts of the partnership. LPs are a little different. While you'll still share in the profits and losses of the partnership, and will be required to report your share of the profits or losses on your personal tax return, you will not be liable for the debts of the partnership. In other words, you'll experience limited liability since the creditors of the partnership are not able to sue the individual partners for the partnership's debts. The most you can lose is your original investment.

How an LP Saves Taxes

LPs have been attractive investments to taxpayers with high marginal tax rates because an LP promises to provide you with a share of the partnership's losses in its start-up years. These losses can either be real losses resulting from start-up costs, or losses generated for tax purposes from writing-off certain amounts, most commonly capital cost allowance (see lesson 92). The losses that are passed along to you can be deducted on your personal tax return, although the amount of loss that can be deducted is limited. The *at-risk rules* in the Income Tax Act will only allow you to deduct losses up to your original cost of the investment (your at-risk amount). Any losses over and above your at-risk amount can be carried forward and used to offset income from the LP in any future year.

Changes that were introduced on April 26, 1995 make it even more difficult to claim losses from LPs where you're not required to contribute your own cash to the LP. You see, many LPs will not require you to come up with the cash to pay for your share of the partnership, rather, they will arrange for these payments to be made out of the profits of the partnership. In most of these types of arrangements, you'll never be required to come up with the cash personally, and so the debt owing to pay for the partnership interest is called *non-recourse debt.* Generally, where non-recourse debt exists, the at-risk amount (the maximum you can deduct with respect to the partnership's losses) will be further reduced by the amount of the non-recourse debt. The rules are complex, so visit your tax professional for more information.

A visit to your tax professional is a good idea any time you're considering an LP investment because you could run into a problem with the *alternative minimum tax (AMT)*. The taxman has said that where you claim large deductions against your income so that the amount of tax you pay is very small, you might be required to pay a certain amount of tax as a minimum – the AMT. To be brief, the amount of your minimum tax will be 17% of your adjusted taxable income over $40,000. Your adjusted taxable income is simply your reported taxable income, plus an add-back of certain deductions you may have taken, including LP losses. You'll also be entitled to your usual non-refundable tax credits, such as the basic personal amount, when calculating your minimum tax. If you've paid AMT, you'll be able to get it back by applying it against regular taxes owing at any time in the next seven years.

The Types of LPs

LP investments can generally be grouped into one of four categories. We'll briefly mention each in a minute, but first, it's important to understand one very important consideration: *the quality of the underlying investment is far more important than any potential tax savings the investment might offer.* Some LPs available are high risk investments, and should only be considered by risk-loving investors. In addition, LPs will generally make your tax return more complex, and you'll probably want to visit a tax professional before making the investment, and perhaps to prepare your return. In our view, while some LPs are decidedly safer than others, there is only one type of LP that is safe enough for most investors looking into these investments: mutual fund limited partnerships, and we'll look at these momentarily.

1. RESOURCE LPs. Mining and oil and gas exploration are areas that can provide tax shelter opportunities through an LP. Investors receive a statement each year detailing some or all of the following: the partnership's business income or loss, the partnership's investment income, your share of Canadian exploration expenses, Canadian development expenses, Canadian oil and gas property expenses, and a resource allowance. Each of these amounts is deductible, to a different degree, on your personal tax return, and forecasts for these expenses should be available to enable proper tax planning. By the way, some provinces offer credits that can be refunded to you for making these investments (Alberta and Saskatchewan for example).

2. FILM LPs. Toronto and Vancouver have become popular sites for television and film producers largely because of the tax treatment afforded producers in Canada. There are a number of LPs available that provide the opportunity to invest in some of these productions. Certified productions will provide either attractive capital cost allowance (CCA) deductions or a tax credit designed to mirror this benefit. At a minimum, even a non-certified production will allow the amount of your investment to be claimed as CCA at a rate of 30% of the remaining unclaimed capital cost each year. Of course, you can imagine how risky some of these investments can be – the production may never be completed for example (and you'll receive no revenue in this case) – so caution should be taken.

3. OTHER BUSINESS LPs. There are LPs available in a number of other businesses. For example, software LPs have become common in the last couple of years. Since the tax legislation permits the write-off of software over what is effectively a two year period, software LPs have offered accelerated deductions to investors. Similarly, LPs are available to enable investment in charter boats, hotels, nursing homes, seismic data and other ventures. Again, these should only be considered to the extent the underlying investments are good ones. While there is potentially significant value to some of these LPs, there can be substantial risk as well, so be careful not to be lured by fast-talking sales people.

4. MFLPs: A GOOD CHOICE. Mutual fund limited partnerships (MFLPs) work this way: certain mutual funds can be purchased by investors without sales charges. These are called *no-load* mutual funds. Similarly, some funds will only charge you a *back-end load*, that is, they will only charge a fee when you get out of the fund. These types of mutual funds can cause a cash problem for the mutual fund company because investment brokers who sell you the mutual funds expect to be paid a commission (about 4%) on the sale at the time the sale is made. To raise cash to pay these commissions, fund companies have come up with the clever idea of an MFLP.

When you buy into an MFLP, your cash is used to pay commissions to brokers selling the mutual funds (there's no need to invest in the mutual fund itself unless you want to). The partnership then receives fees from the mutual fund itself over a number of years (allocated from the management fee), and this income is passed on to you, the individual partner. The fees received by the partnership will be directly related to the market value of the mutual fund itself.

From a tax point of view, Revenue Canada will permit you to deduct your share of the MFLP's commissions that have been paid to investment brokers. Beginning after July 1995, your share of the commissions expense can be deducted equally over three years. This means that, for the first three years you own an interest in an MFLP, you'll have losses to report on your tax return to shelter other income from tax.

MFLPs are attractive because they are as safe as the underlying mutual fund. In our view, these are the safest LPs you could purchase. They are relatively simple to understand, and simple to buy. MFLPs are especially attractive when you have a high marginal tax rate and expect to have a lower marginal rate in the next few years since you'll get losses for the next three years followed by a few years of income. If you'll be retiring in the next five years or so and are currently earning a high income, consider an MFLP. One drawback to MFLPs is that they may not be as liquid as other investments. Be sure to speak to an investment broker and to examine the prospectus before making an investment.

What We Have Learned:

- limited partnerships (LPs) can provide an allocation of losses to you that can be applied against other income, subject to certain limits, to reduce taxable income.
- there are generally four categories of LPs, and mutual fund limited partnerships (MFLPs) are, in our view, the safest.

- *consider an MFLP especially when you currently have a high marginal tax rate but expect that rate to fall over the next few years (this usually happens when you're close to retirement).*

LESSON 119

Consider Labour-Sponsored Venture Capital Corporation shares.

You may have heard about Labour-Sponsored Venture Capital Corporations (LSVCCs) by now. These are special corporations that are designed to provide venture capital to, and promote investment in, developing Canadian businesses. This is how they work: labour unions or employee groups set up a venture capital corporation. These corporations have a mandate to invest in small developing Canadian businesses with good growth potential. Most businesses that will be invested in will be labour-intensive (these provide jobs) or in companies with a high degree of worker participation in management. If you choose to get into one of these LSVCC investments, you'll actually be buying shares in the venture capital corporation.

Investing in an LSVCC is a higher risk investment than most equities, although the risk is reduced by tax credits available. The tax credits are generous: you'll recover up to 40% on the first $5,000 of your investment through federal and provincial tax credits. Unfortunately, the rate of return offered by most LSVCCs has been poor for two reasons: (1) up to 75% of all cash in LSVCCs is currently sitting in low-yielding treasury bills, government bonds, and similar investments[4], and (2) businesses that have been invested in are, by their nature, high risk companies, and it's safe to assume some of these will not be in a position to pay a decent return on the cash advanced to them.

The tax credits available can be attractive, but to take full advantage of them you should not invest more than $5,000 annually in an LSVCC. You see, the credits (federal of $1,000 and provincial of $1,000) total 40% of your invested amount up to a maximum of

---

[4] Many LSVCCs have received criticism in the press recently for being extremely slow to meet their mandate of investing in developing businesses. In many cases, LSVCCs are just 25% to 30% invested with the remainder earning low returns in interest-bearing investments.

$2,000 in total, and you'll reach this maximum credit at an investment of $5,000.

Candice's Credits

Candice heard about the attractive tax credits available when investing in an LSVCC, so she took $5,000 and made an investment in 1996 recommended by her investment broker. Candice received a $1,000 credit ($5,000 x 20%) from the federal government, and another $1,000 credit from the provincial government, for total credits of $2,000. In addition, she transferred her shares of the LSVCC to her RRSP which provided her with a deduction on her tax return of $5,000 for the contribution. The RRSP contribution saved her $2,500 in taxes since her marginal tax rate is 50%. Her total tax savings in 1996 were $4,500 ($2,000 in credits plus $2,500 from the RRSP contribution) on an investment of $5,000.

Candice's story sounds good doesn't it? Invest $5,000 and get $4,500 (90% of your investment) back in tax savings right away. This is the sales pitch you'll get from many investment brokers, but beware, your tax savings from the LSVCC aren't quite as generous as it may appear. The $4,500 in savings includes $2,500 in savings resulting from contributing to your RRSP. The truth is, you would've received the $2,500 in savings no matter what investment you had decided to hold in your RRSP. So, the true savings from the LSVCC investment is just the 40% in credits you'll receive, or $2,000 in Candice's example.

There are some things to watch for if you're considering investing in an LSVCC. First, some LSVCCs are registered federally, and some provincially. All provincially registered LSVCCs provide both a provincial and a federal credit for your investment, but not all federally registered ones offer both credits. In addition, your eligibility for the provincial credits may depend on which province you live in – the rules are complex and change frequently, so be sure to speak to your investment broker. Second, some funds have restrictions on getting your money back: LSVCCs are not mutual funds and are not governed by the same repayment rules that mutual funds operate under. If your LSVCC ever experienced a liquidity problem it would be able to keep your money for up to three months before honouring your redemption request. Lastly, LSVCCs operate under a tax provision that may force you to repay the generous tax credits you received if you redeem your units before a certain time has elapsed since making your investment. Check all the details before handing over your hard-earned money.

What We Have Learned:

- *LSVCCs are a high-risk equity investment supported by generous tax credits available.*
- *never invest more than $5,000 in an LSVCC in a given year since credits are not available beyond this level.*
- *your true tax savings from an LSVCC will be the 40% in tax credits received, not 90% as some suggest.*
- *before buying, check to see that you'll receive both federal and provincial credits, and determine the holding period required before you can get your money back without a penalty.*

LESSON 120

Take advantage of a dividend reinvestment plan where one is offered.

A *dividend reinvestment plan (DRIP)* is a plan that will allow you to buy common or preferred shares in a company that will automatically reinvest any dividends paid to you in more shares of the company. The benefit of this, of course, is that you won't pay any commissions on additional shares issued to you. DRIPs are really a forced investment plan, and before you know it, you'll own much more of the company than you realized.

Danny's DRIP

Danny bought 1,000 common shares of ABC company 10 years ago at $10 per share. ABC company has always offered a dividend reinvestment plan that Danny has taken advantage of over the years, and has consistently paid a dividend of 3% each year. In addition, common shares in ABC have increased in value at an average rate of 10% each year. Even though Danny didn't spend another dime buying shares in ABC company, his 1,000 shares grew to be 1,384 shares after ten years with an aggregate value of $35,903. If he had not been enrolled in the DRIP program, he would've had 1,000 shares after ten years worth an aggregate of $25,940. His investment is nearly $10,000 larger because of the DRIP plan. In *addition, Danny saved brokerage commissions of about $180 over the ten year period – not all that much, but better in his pocket than his broker's.*

When investing in shares of any public company, determine whether the company offers a DRIP plan. If so, be sure to enrol in it; these plans are offered by most utilities, banks, and a variety of other companies. Your broker won't appreciate the DRIP because he won't make commissions on the additions to your account, but after all, it's your money. Don't invest in a stock simply because the company offers a DRIP plan. If the stock is one that you would've otherwise invested in because you like the growth prospects of the company, then a DRIP plan is a bonus, but such a plan won't make an otherwise unattractive stock worth buying. One word of caution: DRIPs may limit your tendency to diversify, so be sure to monitor this.

What We Have Learned:
- *a dividend reinvestment plan (DRIP) allows dividends on shares owned by you to be automatically reinvested in more shares of the company without commissions.*
- *DRIPs are a forced investment plan that you should take advantage of where offered by companies that you would've otherwise invested in.*

LESSON 121

Consider investing in tax-deferred preferred shares.

↓ $

$·$

Tax-deferred preferred shares (TDPSs) were introduced back in lesson 34, point 17. Refer back to that discussion for more information. TDPSs look like bonds, smell like bonds, and the income earned looks an awful lot like interest income, but the good news is that they are called preferred shares, and are taxed as preferred shares. Picture this. You buy a 9 year bond that earns a yield to maturity of 7.42%. The interest income on the bond is earned annually although it's not payable to you until the maturity date of the bond. The interest income is taxed in your hands each year even though you haven't received the cash because you have a *right* to the interest earned (this is the *annual accrual rule* – see lesson 34, point 13). Compare this investment with Paul's.

Paul's Preferreds

Paul heard about some TDPSs issued by Texaco Capital LLC. Paul paid $25 per share for these shares with the hope of deferring taxable income. The shares are redeemable (they can be bought back) and in fact will be redeemed by Texaco in nine years time at a price of $45 per share. If Paul holds the shares until they are redeemed in nine years, he will have earned an average annual yield of 7.42% (same as the bond we just talked about). When the shares are redeemed in nine years, Paul will receive $45 per share, or $20 more per share than the $25 he paid. This $20 per share will be taxed at that time as dividend income. Unlike interest, these dividends are not taxed until Paul actually receives the cash since he doesn't truly have a right to the income until that time. In this case, the dividends are not eligible for the dividend tax credit because Texaco Capital LLC paying the dividends is not a Canadian company. So, the marginal tax rate on these dividends is the same as the marginal rate on interest income (since the dividend tax credit is not available on foreign dividends). Paul's dividends really do look a lot like the interest on the bond we just talked about. The real benefit is that Paul was able to defer tax on his income for nine years, which he couldn't have done with a bond.

The Texaco TDPSs in Paul's example are a real issue of TDPSs that you'll be able to purchase by visiting your investment broker. The only reason we mention them here is that there are very few TDPS issues out there currently, and this is just one that we're aware of. Talk to your broker about the other issues available before deciding on one. In particular, ask whether there are any TDPSs issued by Canadian companies which, unlike Paul's example, may also offer the benefit of the dividend tax credit. If there are such shares available, you'll get the benefit of not only deferring taxable income, but of converting what looks and smells like interest income into dividends, which are taxed at a lower marginal rate.

TDPSs may be best held outside your RRSP when you have investments both inside and outside your plan. The reason for this is that investments inside your RRSP enjoy tax deferral anyway, and so the most attractive feature of these TDPSs is really nothing special inside your RRSP, besides, you may be able to find investments with better rates of return to hold inside your RRSP.

Finally, consider selling your TDPSs before they are redeemed by the issuing company where the dividends to be received on the redemption are not eligible for the dividend tax credit (this is generally the case where the issuing company is not Canadian) and where the shares can be sold for a decent capital gain. By doing this, you'll avoid the foreign dividend which will be taxed at a higher marginal tax rate much like interest, and you'll report a capital gain instead. The capital gain will be taxed at a lower rate than the foreign dividend will be. The only drawback to selling your TDPSs is that you'll pay a commission to your broker on the sale that you wouldn't have paid had you held the shares until their redemption. Note that where the dividends are eligible for the dividend tax credit, they will be taxed at a lower rate than any capital gains will, so hold onto the shares until they are redeemed.

What We Have Learned:
- *tax-deferred preferred shares effectively defer tax until the date the shares are redeemed.*
- *where the dividend tax credit is available on the dividends, you'll effectively convert what looks and smells like interest into dividends, which are taxed at a lower rate.*
- *TDPSs may be best held outside your RRSP, and you should consider selling them before the redemption date where there is no dividend tax credit available.*

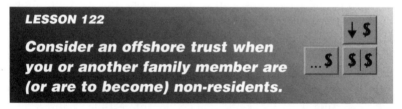

LESSON 122

Consider an offshore trust when you or another family member are (or are to become) non-residents.

If there's one topic that tax professionals are divided on, it's offshore investing[5]. Ask two tax experts what they think about offshore tax planning and you'll get two different answers. One expert will tell you that virtually all offshore tax "planning" is really offshore tax "evasion", while the other will tell you that as long as you dot your i's and cross your t's, you can structure your offshore affairs to avoid tax legally.

---

[5]   Offshore investing does not always involve setting up trusts and corporations in some exotic tax haven. Any time you invest money outside of Canada you're investing offshore, so simply opening a bank account in the United States qualifies as offshore investing.

Our view is that the only safe way to invest is to operate on the basis that Revenue Canada will find out everything it wants to know about your investments. If your offshore structure causes you to fear this premise, maybe you've over-stepped the bound between avoidance and evasion.

We won't get into the many different "borderline" strategies that would be construed by some tax experts as evasion. There are plenty of books out there that will suggest ways to set up an offshore structure that the taxman may take offence to. You should note that, effective January 1, 1996, stringent reporting requirements were introduced by Revenue Canada that will require you to report any amounts transferred to accounts offshore. This will have a significant impact on the investment structures set up by Canadians. We'd like to briefly mention four potential ways to use an offshore trust to save taxes. Before introducing these, let's talk for a minute about income earned offshore and how it's taxed.

Taxation of Your Offshore Income

If you're a resident of Canada for tax purposes, you'll be required to pay tax on your world-wide income. This includes any investment income earned in other parts of the world, including any countries who do not themselves levy taxes on income earned there. If you're hoping to get around this tax problem by earning the money inside a foreign corporation, the idea won't work since the *foreign accrual property income (FAPI) rules* will tax in your hands any investment income that's earned inside a foreign corporation controlled by you. A foreign corporation could be used, however, to defer investment income from tax for a full year, and possibly indefinitely – see lesson 35, point 24. Since you're required to report your world-wide income, saving taxes using an offshore structure can be difficult, and sometimes requires outright evasion to make it work – which means, in reality, it doesn't work. There are some planning opportunities available, however, by using a trust in certain situations.

Offshore Trusts: Four Scenarios

First of all, an offshore trust won't always save you tax dollars. In fact, investment income earned inside an offshore trust will be taxed by Revenue Canada if two tests are met (these are simplified here): (1) you or another Canadian resident have any current or future right to income or capital of the trust, either directly or indirectly, and (2) the trust acquires property from a Canadian resident who is beneficially interested in the trust, or related to such a person. The following four scenarios may provide opportunities for you to use offshore trusts to save taxes.

1. CREATE AN OFFSHORE TRUST TO BENEFIT A NON-RESIDENT. If you have any family members living, for example, in the U.S., you could set up an offshore trust that would effectively provide income to those family members tax-free provided you're not a U.S. citizen or green card holder, and the trust qualifies as a *grantor trust* under U.S. law. Distributions out of such a trust would be considered tax-free gifts by the IRS as long as these are not distributions of tangible property located in the U.S.

2. HAVE A NON-RESIDENT SET UP A TRUST. If you're able to get on the good side of a wealthy family member who happens to be a non-resident for Canadian tax purposes, he or she could set up a trust in a tax haven with you as a beneficiary. The trust could earn investment income and make periodic distributions to you on a tax-free basis if it qualifies as a personal trust under Canadian law. Be sure to point this out to any non-resident relative from whom you expect to receive an inheritance.

3. SET UP AN IMMIGRANT OFFSHORE TRUST. Someone moving to Canada is able, under Canadian tax law, to set up an offshore trust before coming to Canada and shelter any income earned in the trust from Canadian tax for the first 60 months of residency in Canada. It doesn't matter whether or not the beneficiaries are already Canadian residents, there will be no tax on the accumulating income for the first 60 months.

4. SET UP A TRUST BEFORE LEAVING CANADA. If you've decided to leave Canada, perhaps to retire down south, consider setting up an offshore trust with your Canadian relatives as beneficiaries. Any income earned in the trust will be taxable in Canada for any years or part-years in which you were still a Canadian resident, but starting in your first full year of residency elsewhere, the income will grow inside the trust and can be periodically distributed to your Canadian resident family members as tax-free capital. For example, if you set up an offshore trust in 1996 and leave for the sunny south in November of 1997, the trust income will be taxable in Canada for

1996 and 1997, but after that, income accumulated will not be taxed in Canada, and tax-free distributions can be made to Canadian residents.

There are other much more complicated structures which can be set up on a case by case basis. If you want to investigate these, a visit to your tax professional or to someone specializing in this field is a good idea.

What We Have Learned:

- *Canadian residents are taxed on world-wide income, including investment income earned offshore in a tax haven whether earned personally or through a corporation.*
- *some offshore investment structures border on evasion.*
- *there are four clear scenarios in which offshore trusts can be used to save taxes; others are beyond the scope of this book.*
- *these scenarios generally require the involvement of an individual who is a non-resident for Canadian tax purposes.*

LESSON 123

Improve cash flow by investing in a back to back prescribed annuity.

... $

If you're over 65 years of age and have money invested outside an RRSP or RRIF that provides you with income for daily living, a back to back prescribed annuity could significantly increase your cash flow and provide the same security for your money. A back to back simply involves purchasing a prescribed annuity plus term insurance. A couple of examples should help to illustrate. Our friend Floyd represents the typical senior, while Alice has taken advantage of a back to back prescribed annuity.

Floyd's Income

Floyd is 70 years old. He currently has $100,000 invested in 7.5% GICs which provide him with about $7,500 in income each year. He has other pension income, and his marginal tax rate is 50%, so he'll pay $3,750 in taxes on this GIC income, and will be left with $3,750 each year to use for daily living. Floyd likes the GICs because he can live off the interest generated without ever dipping into his $100,000 capital, and so he'll be able *to leave the $100,000 to his children when he passes away. Floyd, like many seniors, had never heard of a back to back prescribed annuity – until he spoke with his friend Alice.*

While Floyd's investment in GICs will successfully preserve his $100,000 capital, the interest income is highly taxed, and so he's left with very little (just $3,750) each year. Alice has done better for herself. Here's her story.

Alice's Back to Back

Alice is in the same position as Floyd. She is also 70 years of age and has $100,000 that used to be invested in GICs providing the same $3,750 after-taxes that Floyd receives. Alice is now invested in a back to back prescribed annuity. It works this way: Alice used her $100,000 to buy a prescribed life annuity that will pay her $12,491 a year. The tax on the annuity will only be $2,077 each year since only a portion of the annuity payments are taxable. You see, each annuity payment is made up of interest income plus a return of capital, and only some of the initial interest portion is taxable, so Alice's taxes are fairly low. After taxes, Alice is left with $10,414 ($12,491-$2,077) which is much higher than the $3,750 she was receiving each year with the GICs. The drawback? Each time Alice receives an annuity payment, she's getting back some of her original $100,000 capital, so that she won't be able to leave her children the $100,000 that she could have with the GICs. In fact, when she dies, the remainder of her $100,000 technically goes to the insurance company. No problem – with the extra cash she's receiving, Alice is able to buy a term-to-100 life insurance policy that will pay her children $100,000 when she dies. The cost of the policy will be about $3,281 each year. So Alice takes the $10,414 she has been receiving after taxes, pays her insurance premiums of $3,281, and is still left with $7,133 in her pocket each year. This $7,133 is a full $3,383 more than the $3,750 of after-tax income she used to receive on her GICs.

The idea we've just described is called a back to back prescribed annuity because it involves buying both a life annuity and an insurance policy back to back. Visit your life insurance agent if you're interested in this idea, but ask your agent first if he or she is familiar with this idea.

What We Have Learned:
- *a back to back prescribed annuity involves buying a life annuity to provide increased cash flow and then buying a term-to-100 life insurance policy to provide your family with the same money that they would've received upon your death had you kept your money in GICs or similar investments.*
- *see your insurance broker to set up a back to back.*

LESSON 124

Combine a back to back prescribed annuity with equity mutual funds.

If you've decided to invest in a back to back prescribed annuity (see our last lesson), then consider taking the idea one step further. When you buy the back to back, use some of your funds to invest in equity mutual funds to protect yourself against inflation and provide an emergency fund. You see, when you buy a life annuity, the interest rate is locked-in at the start, and further, it's a very expensive option to arrange for annuity payments that increase each year with inflation (indexed annuity payments). A solution is to invest only a portion of your capital in a back to back prescribed annuity (enough to beat the cash flow you would've received from a GIC), and invest the rest in equity mutual funds which serve as an excellent hedge against inflation, reduce tax exposure by converting income to capital gains and dividends, and are liquid so that you'll have extra cash available for emergencies or other purchases.

George's Back to Back Plus

George is in the same boat as Alice in our last lesson. He had $100,000 invested in GICs until he heard about back to back prescribed annuities. George had been receiving $3,750 in after-tax income from his GICs, just like Alice. George used $60,000 of his money to buy a back to back which provides him with $4,749 in after-tax income each year which is less than Alice's $7,133, but is still more than the $3,750 he used to receive. Even better, George still has $40,000 to invest in equity mutual funds to protect himself against inflation. In addition, if he ever wanted to use some of the $40,000, he could easily access it, unlike the money in the life annuity which is locked-in to make the annuity payments. At first, George was worried about his $40,000 being invested in equity mutual funds because they are more risky than some other investments, but because of his annuity, he is guaranteed a cash flow that beats his GIC, so his concerns were laid to rest.

What We Have Learned:
• **where you invest in a back to back prescribed annuity but want protection from inflation and an emergency fund available, consider combining the back to back with an investment in equity mutual funds.**

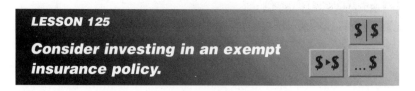

LESSON 125

Consider investing in an exempt insurance policy.

There are basically two types of insurance policies: term and whole-life. When you buy *term insurance* you're buying pure insurance, and nothing more. The cost of term insurance is based on the probability of your death for someone of your age, consequently, premiums on a term policy usually increase as you get older. Term is the cheapest type of insurance, and must be renewed every few years. Most policies will guarantee renewal without a medical exam as long as you continue to pay your premiums, and term policies are not usually renewable past age 75 or so (term-to-100 policies are an exception).

Whole-life insurance will provide coverage for your lifetime. The premiums are higher for a policy of this type, although they are usually constant (no increases) for the time you're paying premiums. Whole-life policies have two components to them: (1) an insurance component, and (2) an investment (cash value) component. The investment component arises because the true cost of insurance on your life is less than the premiums you're paying in the earlier years of the policy.

Exempt Insurance Policies
Most whole-life policies are designed to qualify as *exempt policies* under the Income Tax Act. The benefit of an exempt policy is that

the investment portion of the policy is allowed to grow tax-free. In order to qualify as an exempt policy, the investment portion of your policy must not exceed certain limits, but don't worry about this issue because it's the responsibility of your insurance company to make sure your policy qualifies as exempt.

Exempt policies will allow your money to grow on a tax-free basis until one of the following happens: you borrow from the accumulating investments, you receive dividends from the policy, or you completely or partially surrender the policy. Before doing any of these things, be sure to determine the tax consequences first.

Upon your death, the face value of the policy, plus the value of the accumulated investments, will be paid out to your beneficiaries tax-free. As a result, these policies can effectively defer or eliminate tax altogether, as we mentioned in lessons 33 and 46.

Exempt policies are worth considering only after you've maximized your RRSP contributions since the RRSP is less complex, it offers the same deferral, and you'll be able to access your money easier in the RRSP. The RRSP, of course, won't be paid out tax-free to your beneficiaries like the exempt policy will, unless the beneficiary is your spouse or a dependent child (see lesson 67). By the way, while the funds in the exempt policy are clearly available to your beneficiaries after your death, there are ways of accessing these funds while you're still alive, albeit at a variety of different tax or interest costs.

Before jumping at the chance to invest in an exempt policy, find out how much you're paying for the insurance portion of the product. Where the cost of the insurance is close to what you'd pay under a term policy with the same face value, you'll do well to invest in an exempt policy assuming you'd like to leave your family some tax-free capital. Be sure to shop around since prices can vary for what is essentially the same product.

What We Have Learned:

- *there are basically two types of insurance: term and whole-life.*
- *most whole-life policies qualify as exempt insurance policies that will allow the investment component to grow tax-free until cash values are withdrawn from the policy.*
- *upon death, the face value plus accumulated investments will be paid tax-free to your beneficiaries.*

- *determine the cost of the insurance component under the policy, and shop around for the best prices.*
- *maximize your RRSP contributions first, then consider an exempt life insurance policy.*

LESSON 126

Enter into a commodity straddle.

This investment concept is not for the faint-hearted. If you don't mind the possibility of Revenue Canada applying the general anti-avoidance rule (see lesson 6) to disallow this strategy, maybe it would be fun to give it a try. But first, a brief lesson on what a futures contract is.

Futures Contracts

A futures contract is simply a legally binding commitment to deliver, or *take delivery* of, a certain commodity at an agreed date in the future and at a price set today. For example, you might enter into a contract to take delivery of 100 ounces of gold next February at a price of $370 per ounce. In 98% of futures contracts, delivery of the actual commodity never actually happens. Instead, investors sell their contracts before the delivery date hoping to make a profit. In our example, what would happen to our futures contract if February was approaching and the price of gold shot up to $400? Don't forget, the contract offers the right to take delivery of gold at just $370, so if gold is worth $400 but we can take delivery for a cost of just $370, then the contract becomes quite valuable. In fact, we could sell the contract itself (not the gold – just the contract) for more than we paid for it. As the price of gold rises, the value of our futures contract rises.

We could also purchase a contract giving us the right to *deliver* gold next February at a price of $370. In this case, the opposite happens: as the price of gold rises, the value of our contract falls. After all, what good is the right to deliver gold for $370 an ounce when you should be able to deliver it for $400 an ounce – the current market value.

The Commodity Straddle

What is a commodity straddle? It's where you purchase two futures contracts in a particular commodity: one offers the right to take delivery on a certain date for a certain price (a buy position), and the other offers the right to deliver the same commodity at the same price on the same date (a sell position). Ideally, you should make sure that the positions are not perfectly offsetting in order to provide a reason other than taxation for entering the contract – the taxman doesn't always like transactions that are strictly tax-motivated. By the time December rolls around, one of the futures contracts will have an accrued loss while the other should have an accrued gain since the price of the commodity will have changed since entering the contracts. By selling the contract with the loss before year end you can use the loss to offset income in that year. Shortly after year end, sell the contract with the accrued gain. What you've done is deferred income from one year to the next.

Scott's Straddle

In June 1996 Scott purchased a futures contract for $3,000 to take delivery of 100 ounces of gold at $370 per ounce in February 1997. At the same time, he purchased a contract for $3,000 giving him the right to deliver 100 ounces of gold at $370 per ounce, also in February 1997. On December 30, 1996, gold had risen to $390 per ounce with the result that Scott's buy position had increased in value while his sell position had fallen in value (Scott doesn't care if the price rises or falls, just that it moves enough to make this idea effective). Scott sold his sell position at a $2,000 loss on December 30, 1996 and applied the loss against his other sources of income in 1996. On January 2, 1997, Scott sold his buy position at a $2,000 profit which he will include in his income for 1997. From a tax perspective, Scott has reduced his 1996 income by $2,000 and moved this income into 1997 – he has deferred income for one year.

A commodity straddle can also be used to split taxable income. Here's how: rather than buying both contracts yourself, just buy the losing contract and have your lower-income spouse buy the profitable contract. You'll get the deduction for the loss while your spouse will get the inclusion in income the next year. The only problem, of course, is guessing at the outset which of the contracts will be the loser and which will be the winner – you'll have to make an educated guess at which way the commodity's price is going to move. This can be a risky proposition since, if you guess wrong, you'll end up worse off because you'll get an income inclusion and your lower-income spouse will get the deduction – a bad deal.

It's important to note that, in Scott's example, he sold his profitable contract four days after selling the loser and made a profit in 1997 exactly equal to the loss in 1996. In reality, the price of your commodity could move between the selling of the first and second contracts. So there's the risk that the profit on your second contract will not completely offset the loss on the first contract. In addition, our example has ignored the fact that Scott would've paid commissions to his broker on the sale of the contracts. These are things you'll have to consider before trying this idea.

What We Have Learned:

- *a commodity straddle involves simultaneously purchasing buy and sell futures positions in the same commodity.*
- *selling the losing contract before year end and the other immediately after year end can result in deferring tax by shifting income from one year to the next.*
- *a commodity straddle can also be used to split taxable income, but this is a more risky idea.*

LESSON 127

Invest in a Canadian Controlled Private Corporation.

An investment in the shares or debt of a *Canadian Controlled Private Corporation (CCPC)* by a Canadian resident investor has attractive tax advantages. If the company does well, the value of your shares are sure to increase, and the increase could be substantial. It's not uncommon, for example, for a shareholder to pay $10 for shares in a newly formed company and to find those same shares worth anywhere from $100,000 to over $1 million in a matter of a few years, and sometimes sooner. Unlike any other investment a Canadian can make, the first $500,000 in gains on shares in a qualifying CCPC can be exempt from tax. This is possible due to the enhanced capital gains exemption which, unlike the $100,000 lifetime exemption, is still available to investors (see lesson 16).

What if your investment goes sour? Certainly there's the possibility that a CCPC could fail. In fact, a high percentage of new private businesses close their doors for good within five years of starting up. In this event, a portion of any shares or debt that you hold can be written off as an *allowable business investment loss (ABIL)* in most cases (see lesson 13).

Finding a CCPC

Where do these companies exist? Anywhere from your basement on up. Virtually every type of business with a reasonable expectation of profit can become a CCPC simply by incorporating the business. Don't jump into incorporation right away; it's best to wait until the business has grown in size and profitability (see lesson 100).

If you'd like to invest in someone else's CCPC, there are currently two major investment networks operating in Canada which match fledgling, private companies in a variety of over 25 different industries to investors interested in the companies. Generally, you'll need $10,000 or more to be able to make an investment. These services will simply introduce you to potential CCPCs; all deals are the responsibility of you and the other party to negotiate, and so your investment can take almost any form: equity, debt or any other agreed scenario.

The first of these networks is the *Canada Opportunities Investor Network (COIN)* which is a project of Provincial Chambers of Commerce across Canada and managed by VentureLinx Canada (phone 1-800-931-1002). The second, *The Investment Exchange* (phone 403-299-1770), is based in Calgary, and is a private organization that matches investors and corporations in both Canada and the United States.

What We Have Learned:

- *investing in a CCPC can offer significant tax advantages due to the enhanced capital gains exemption available.*
- *even when the business fails, an ABIL may be available to offset other income.*
- *investing in a CCPC can be done by incorporating your own business or by contacting one of two network organizations that match investors with companies looking for money.*

Last Word

You have the right to pay the least amount of tax that the law will allow, and now you're equipped to do just that. Each of the ideas introduced in this book is a stone in the wall between you and the taxman - a wall that will keep Revenue Canada out of your pockets. So the next step is for you to actually implement some of the ideas that we've introduced - we'd encourage you to use the strategies that apply to your circumstances, and to get professional tax advice for the more complex tax planning ideas.

In closing, our tax system has its problems, and if you find any of the facts, figures, or tax rules in this book disturbing and in need of change, we'd encourage you to contact your MP to challenge him or her to make changes to our tax system. And if you take it upon yourself to do this, we'd appreciate receiving a copy of your correspondence - our address is inside the title page at the front.

Until we meet again...happy tax-savings!

Appendices

Revenue   Revenu
Canada   Canada

DECLARATION OF TAXPAYER RIGHTS

YOU ARE ENTITLED TO A FAIR HEARING AND COURTEOUS TREATMENT. FAIR HANDLING OF A COMPLAINT IS ONE OF YOUR FUNDAMENTAL RIGHTS. ONE OF OUR OBLIGATIONS IS TO HELP YOU EXERCISE YOUR RIGHTS.

IN YOUR DEALINGS WITH REVENUE CANADA ON INCOME TAX MATTERS, YOU HAVE IMPORTANT RIGHTS

Information
You are entitled to complete and accurate information about the *Income Tax Act,* the entitlements it allows you, and the obligations it imposes on you.

Courtesy and consideration
You are entitled to courteous and considerate treatment in all your dealings with us, whether we are requesting information or arranging for an interview or an audit.

Impartiality
You are entitled to demand impartial application of the law. It is our job to collect only the correct amount of tax, no more and no less.

Presumption of honesty
You are entitled to be presumed honest unless there is evidence to the contrary.

Privacy and confidentiality
You are entitled to expect that we will use the personal and financial information you provide us only for purposes the law allows.

YOU ARE ENTITLED TO MANY OTHER RIGHTS UNDER THE LAWS OF CANADA.

Disputed amounts
You are entitled to withhold disputed amounts, to the extent the law allows, until our officers or a court decides on your objection. If you appeal to a higher court, you can put up security instead of paying the disputed amounts.

Impartial review
You are entitled to object to an assessment if you believe you have been treated unfairly. You must exercise this right within a specific period. Once you have filed a notice of objection, we will conduct an impartial review of your file. If the matter is not resolved to your satisfaction, you can appeal to the courts.

Bilingual service
You are entitled to service in the official language of your choice.

YOU ARE ENTITLED TO KNOW YOUR RIGHTS AND TO INSIST THAT THEY BE RESPECTED.

YOU HAVE THE RIGHT TO EVERY BENEFIT THE LAW ALLOWS
You are entitled to arrange your affairs to pay the least amount of tax the law allows. We are committed to applying the tax laws in a consistent and fair manner. We will be firm with those who are guilty of tax evasion.

Canadä

APPENDIX 2

COMBINED FEDERAL & PROVINCIAL MARGINAL TAX RATES (%)				
1996 Taxable Income	$6,457- 29,590	$29,591- 59,180	$59,181- 62,195	$62,196 and over
British Columbia				
Interest and Salary	26.4	41.2	49.7	54.2
Dividends	7.1	24.6	33.5	36.5
Capital Gains	19.8	30.9	37.3	40.6
Alberta				
Interest and Salary	25.8	39.6	44.6	46.1
Dividends	7.4	24.1	30.4	31.4
Capital Gains	19.3	29.7	33.5	34.6
Saskatchewan				
Interest and Salary	29.1	44.8	50.5	51.9
Dividends	10.0	28.4	35.5	36.5
Capital Gains	21.8	33.6	37.9	39.0
Manitoba				
Interest and Salary	28.4	44.3	49.0	50.4
Dividends	9.6	29.5	35.4	36.3
Capital Gains	21.3	33.2	36.7	37.8
Ontario				
Interest and Salary	27.5	42.7	50.1	53.2
Dividends	7.5	25.5	33.8	35.9
Capital Gains	20.6	32.0	37.5	39.9
Quebec				
Interest and Salary	34.5	47.2	51.5	52.9
Dividends	18.3	32.9	37.7	38.7
Capital Gains	25.9	35.4	38.6	39.7

Note:

Some rates in some provinces may differ slightly due to provincial surtaxes on income thresholds between those indicated. The rates shown are average rates where these secondary thresholds exist.

APPENDIX 2

COMBINED FEDERAL & PROVINCIAL MARGINAL TAX RATES (%)				
1996 Taxable Income	$6,457- 29,590	$29,591- 59,180	$59,181- 62,195	$62,196 and over
New Brunswick				
Interest and Salary	28.4	43.4	48.4	51.3
Dividends	7.7	26.4	32.7	34.7
Capital Gains	21.3	32.6	36.3	38.5
Nova Scotia				
Interest and Salary	27.6	42.2	48.9	53.7
Dividends	7.4	25.7	33.7	36.3
Capital Gains	20.7	31.7	37.9	40.3
Prince Edward Island				
Interest and Salary	27.6	42.2	47.1	50.3
Dividends	7.4	25.7	31.8	33.9
Capital Gains	20.7	31.7	35.3	37.7
Newfoundland				
Interest and Salary	29.2	44.7	49.9	51.3
Dividends	7.9	27.2	33.7	34.7
Capital Gains	21.9	33.5	37.4	38.5
Yukon				
Interest and Salary	26.0	39.8	44.8	46.5
Dividends	7.0	24.2	30.2	31.4
Capital Gains	19.5	29.8	33.8	34.9
Northwest Territories				
Interest and Salary	25.2	38.5	42.9	44.4
Dividends	6.8	23.4	29.0	30.0
Capital Gains	18.9	28.9	32.2	33.3

Note:

Some rates in some provinces may differ slightly due to provincial surtaxes on income thresholds between those indicated. The rates shown are average rates where these secondary thresholds exist.

APPENDIX 3

FEDERAL PERSONAL TAX RATES FOR 1996	
Taxable Income Level	**Amount of Tax**
$ — to $ 29,590	17% of income
$ 29,591 to $ 59,180	$5,030 + 26% on income over $29,590
$ 59,181 and over	$12,724 + 29% on income over $59,180

Notes:

(1)   A surtax of 3% of basic federal tax is added after taking into account personal tax credits (see Appendix 5), dividend tax credits, and forward averaging tax credits that apply.

(2)   An additional surtax of 5% of basic federal tax will apply where basic federal tax, after applicable credits and before the 3% surtax, is in excess of $12,500.

APPENDIX 4

PROVINCIAL PERSONAL TAX RATES FOR 1996		
Province	Tax Rate: % of Basic Federal Tax	
British Columbia	52.5	(1)
Alberta	45.5	(2)
Saskatchewan	50.0	(3)
Manitoba	52.0	(4)
Ontario	58.0	(5)
Quebec	see note	(6)
New Brunswick	64.0	(7)
Nova Scotia	59.5	(8)
Prince Edward Island	59.5	(9)
Newfoundland	69.0	
Northwest Territories	45.0	
Yukon Territory	50.0	(10)
Non-resident	52.0	

Notes:

(1) A surtax of 30% applies to B.C. tax exceeding $5,300. An additional surtax of 20% applies to B.C. tax exceeding $9,000.

(2) A surtax of 8% of basic Alberta tax in excess of $3,500 and a flat tax of 0.5% of Alberta taxable income are levied.

(3) There is a flat tax of 2% of net income and a surtax of 15% on Saskatchewan tax (including flat tax) in excess of $4,000. An additional *Debt Reduction Surtax* of 10% applies to basic Saskatchewan tax plus the flat tax. Effective July 1, 1995, the debt reduction surtax will be eliminated or reduced for lower-income earners - an annual reduction against the surtax of up to $150 per tax-payer and up to $300 per dual-income household will be provided.

(4) A flat tax of 2% of net income and a surtax equal to 2% of net income in excess of $30,000 are levied in Manitoba.

(5) A surtax of 20% applies to Ontario tax exceeding $5,500 plus an additional surtax of 10% on Ontario tax exceeding $8,000.

APPENDIX 4 (continued)

Notes:

(6)   Quebec Personal Tax Rates for 1996:

Taxable Income Level			Amount of Tax
Nil	to	$ 7,000	16% of income
$ 7,001	to	$14,000	$ 1,120 + 19% over $7,000
$14,001	to	$23,000	$ 2,450 + 21% over $14,000
$23,001	to	$50,000	$ 4,340 + 23% over $23,000
$50,001	and	over	$10,550 + 24% over $50,000

Residents of Quebec receive a reduction of their federal taxes equal to 16.5% of Basic Federal Tax. Quebec imposes a surtax of 5% of Quebec tax exceeding $5,000 plus 5% of Quebec tax exceeding $10,000. A tax reduction is granted equal to 2% of the excess of $10,000 over tax payable after deducting non-refundable tax credits. This tax reduction declines as taxes payable approach $10,000.

(7)   A surtax of 8% applies to basic New Brunswick tax in excess of $13,500.

(8)   A surtax of 10% on Nova Scotia tax in excess of $10,000 is levied.

(9)   A surtax of 10% applies to basic P.E.I. tax in excess of $12,500.

(10) A surtax of 5% applies to Yukon Territory tax in excess of $6,000.

Reprinted from the Practitioner's Income Tax Act, 8th Edition, August 1995, by permission of Carswell, a division of Thomson Canada Limited.

APPENDIX 5

| | PERSONAL TAX CREDITS FOR 1996 | | | | |
| | COMBINED FEDERAL AND PROVINCIAL VALUES | | | | |
Jurisdiction	Basic Personal Amount	(1) (2) Married or Equiv- alent	(1) Depend- ants Credits	(3) Age Am- ount for over 65	(3) (4) Disabili- ty Tax Credit
Federal	$1,098	$ 915	$ 269	$ 592	$ 720
British Columbia	1,707	1,423	418	921	1,120
Alberta	1,631	1,359	399	879	1,069
Saskatchewan	1,680	1,400	412	906	1,102
Manitoba	1,702	1,418	417	918	1,116
Ontario	1,768	1,473	433	953	1,159
Quebec (5)	1,180	1,180	1,180	440	440
New Brunswick	1,834	1,528	449	989	1,202
Nova Scotia	1,784	1,487	437	962	1,170
P.E.I.	1,784	1,487	437	962	1,170
Newfoundland	1,889	1,574	463	1,018	1,238
Northwest Territories	1,625	1,354	398	876	1,066
Yukon Territory	1,680	1,400	412	906	1,102

Notes:

The federal tax credit values and credit percentages do not include the basic 3% federal surtax savings, or the additional 5% high income surtax, and are before the federal tax abatement available to residents of Quebec.

The combined federal and provincial credit values and credit percentages reflect the basic federal tax, low-rate federal surtax, and provincial tax, but do not reflect either the high income federal surtax or any provincial surtaxes or flat taxes.

APPENDIX 5 (continued)

Notes:

(1) The value of the credit is reduced by the result of applying the credit reduction rate to the dependant's net income in excess of $538 for married/equivalent-to-spouse and $2,690 for other dependants.

(2) Eligible dependants for the equivalent-to-spouse credit are dependants under age 18 related to the taxpayer, or the taxpayer's parents/grandparents, or any other person who is related to the taxpayer and is infirm.

(3) These credits are transferable to a spouse. The credits available for transfer are reduced by the amount resulting from the application of the credit reduction rate to the transferor's net income in excess of $6,456. The age amount will be clawed back for seniors with incomes over $25,921 and will disappear completely at an income level of $49,134.

(4) These credits are transferable to a supporting parent or grandparent. The transferable credit is reduced by the amount resulting from the application of the credit reduction rate to the transferor's net income in excess of $6,456.

(5) The amounts shown below are the 1996 credit values and credit percentages for Quebec provincial income tax purposes and are adjusted as follows:
- the married and dependent credits are reduced by the lesser of the available credit amount and 20% of the dependant's earnings
- the equivalent-to-spouse credit is nil, but a single parent may claim a credit of $260
- the person living-alone credit is $210
- the credit for the first dependant child is $520
- the credit for a second and subsequent dependent children is $480
- the credit for other dependants is $450; $1,180 if disabled
- the credit for support of eligible direct ascendants is $550
- the education credit is $330 per term, a maximum of $600 per year
- tuition fees are deductible against income for Quebec tax purposes
- a new refundable credit for "adoption expenses" was introduced in the 1994 Quebec budget equal to 20% of eligible adoption expenses to a maximum credit of $1,000.

Reprinted from the Practitioner's Income Tax Act, 8th Edition, August 1995, by permission of Carswell, a division of Thomson Canada Limited.

APPENDIX 6

MINIMUM ANNUAL RRIF WITHDRAWALS (%)		
Age	General	Pre-1993 Qualifying RRIFs
65	4.00	4.00
66	4.17	4.17
67	4.35	4.35
68	4.55	4.55
69	4.76	4.76
70	5.00	5.00
71	7.38	5.26
72	7.48	5.56
73	7.59	5.88
74	7.71	6.25
75	7.85	6.67
76	7.99	7.14
77	8.15	7.69
78	8.33	8.33
79	8.53	8.53
80	8.75	8.75
81	8.99	8.99
82	9.27	9.27
83	9.58	9.58
84	9.93	9.93
85	10.33	10.33
86	10.79	10.79
87	11.33	11.33
88	11.96	11.96
89	12.71	12.71
90	13.62	13.62
91	14.73	14.73
92	16.12	16.12
93	17.92	17.92
94 or older	20.00	20.00

Note: The minimum annual withdrawal from a RRIF equals the balance of investments inside the RRIF at the start of the year multiplied by the above percentages. RRIFs established prior to 1993 are called qualifying RRIFs and annuitants should use the right column above. Your age for this calculation is your age at the very start of January 1st of any given year. If you're under age 65, the formula to calculate the percentage for your minimum annual withdrawal is as follows: $1/(90$ minus your age) = percentage for minimum withdrawal.

APPENDIX 7

COMMON CAPITAL COST ALLOWANCE (CCA) CLASSES AND RATES		
Capital Asset	**CCA Class**	**(1) CCA Rate (%)**
Automobiles	10 or 10.1	30 (2)
Furniture and fixtures	8	20
Computer hardware	10	30 (3)
Computer software	12	100 (4)
Other office equipment	8	20
Tools costing under $200	12	100 (5)
Buildings aquired after 1987	1	4
Buildings aquired 1979 - 1987	3	5

Notes:

(1) In the year of acquisition, only one half of the CCA based on the above rates may be claimed.

(2) Automobiles with a cost of $24,000 or more (excluding GST and PST) will be placed in class 10.1. Others will be class 10. The amount included in the class will be the cost of the car plus PST for class 10 assets, and $24,000 plus PST for class 10.1 assets.

(3) Computer hardware includes systems software.

(4) Computer software includes applications software only.

(5) Such tools are not subject to the half-year rule in point 1 above.

The Capital Cost Allowance classes and rates occupy 25 full pages in the Income Tax Act - this should give you an appreciation for the diversity and complexity of the CCA rules. See a tax professional if your situation is at all unique.

A

Advice
    on investments, 183
    on taxes, 13
Aircraft expenses. *See* Deductions
Alimony payments, 57
Allowable business investment loss.
    See Losses
Allowance
    non-taxable, for auto, 19
    non-taxable, travel, 19
Alternative Minimum Tax, 65, 192
Annual accrual rule. *See* Interest
    income
Annuity
    life annuity, 63, 96, 131
    maturing RRSP, 115, 131
    prescribed, 67, 203, 205
    qualified RRSP investment, 110
    tax-free receipts, 87
    term-certain, 64, 67, 96
Artist's costs. *See* Deductions
At-risk rules, 191
Attendant costs. *See* Deductions
Attribution rules, 45
Automobile expenses. *See*
    Deductions
Avoidance. *See* Tax avoidance

B

Bankruptcy, 96
Basic personal amount. *See* Credits
Benefits
    death, 41
    non-taxable, 36
    taxable, 41
Business losses. *See* Self-employ-
    ment losses

C

Canada Deposit Insurance. *See*
    Insurance
Canada pension plan, 56, 95, 166
Canadian Controlled Private
    Corporation, 71, 210
Capital assets, 19, 152
Capital cost allowance. *See*
    Deductions
Capital gains
    applying losses against, 30, 53,
        158
    capital gains exempt balance,
        190
    inside RRSP, 81
    investments giving rise to, 174,
        175
    mutual funds, from, 31
    non-qualified investments, on,
        125
    reserve available, 69
    taxed in the U.S., 144
    transferring to children, 49
    versus business income, 32
    versus other income, 78, 200
Capital gains exemption
    enhanced exemption, 29, 80,
        210
    lifetime exemption, 29, 79, 210
Capital losses. *See* Losses
Capital property, 10, 11, 48, 51, 68,
    69, 88, 158
Capital versus income, 32
Carrying charges. *See* Deductions
CCPC. *See* Canadian Controlled
    Private Corporation
Charitable donations, 9, 52
Child care costs. *See* Deductions
Child tax benefits, 54
Clergy residence. *See* Deductions
Clothing
    non-taxable benefit, 38, 40
Commissions
    brokers, paid to, 184, 186, 194
    deductions against, 19

non-taxable benefit, 38
Commodity straddle, 208
Common shares, 58, 77, 79, 82, 197
Consulting. *See* Self-employment
Convertible debentures, 85
Converting taxable income. *See* Pillars of tax planning
Corporations. *See* Incorporation
Counselling
  non-taxable benefit, 37
Creditors, 96
Credits
  basic personal amount, 121, 137, 159
  compared to deductions, 8
  CPP contributions, for, 167
  dividend tax credit, 59, 199
  foreign tax credits, 144
  instalments, for, 169
  investment tax credits, 160
  medical expenses, 52
  pension income, for, 132
  rent, for, 47
  spouse, for, 57
  transfer to spouse, 52, 133

D

Day-care
  costs deductible. *See* Child care costs
  non-taxable benefit, 38
Death
  establishing liability today, 58
  income from deceased spouse, 133
  leaving a retiring allowance, 65
  leaving property to family, 51
  leaving RRSP funds, 115
  life insurance, 66, 86, 206
  planning for taxes, 11
  RRSP contributions after, 122
Death benefit. *See* Benefits
Debt forgiveness rules, 48
Deductions

aircraft expenses, 20, 44
artist's costs, 20
attendant costs, 20
automobile expenses, 19, 44, 155
capital cost allowance, 20, 151, 152, 155, 191, 193
carrying charges, 22
child care costs, 24
clergy residence, 20
compared to credits, 8
employees, available to, 19
home office, 19, 34, 153, 157
interest costs, 20, 22, 43, 46, 48, 105, 154, 155, 157
lease costs, 155
legal costs, 20
meals and entertainment, 156
membership dues, 20
moving expenses, 23
rent, 20
salaries and wages, 20, 58, 156, 162, 163
salesperson, 19
supplies, 19
transfer to spouse, 52
travel costs, 19
Deferred Profit Sharing Plans, 64
Deferring taxable income. *See* Pillars of tax planning
Dental plan
  non-taxable benefit, 39
Depreciation. *See* Capital cost allowance
Disabled persons. *See* attendant costs
Discounts for employees
  non-taxable benefit, 38
Dividend income
  foreign dividends, 200
  high yields available, 83
  inside RRSP, 81
  insurance policies, from, 207
  investments giving rise to, 174, 175
  mutual funds, from, 31

postpone payment of, 74
tax-deferred shares, from, 70,
    198
tax-free, 59
transfer to spouse, 57
versus other income, 78
Dividend re-investment plans, 186,
197
Dividend tax credit. *See* Credits
Divorce, 10
Donations. *See* Charitable donations

E

Earned income. *See* Registered
    Retirement Savings Plans
Education costs
    non-taxable benefit, 39
Effective tax rate. *See* Tax rates
Emigrating from Canada
    RRSP considerations, 141
    setting up trust prior to, 200
    tax advice, 11, 13
    transferring property prior to, 51
Employee deductions. *See*
    Deductions
Employee loans. *See* Loans
Entertainment expenses
    deductible, 156
Estate freeze, 58
Evasion. *See* Tax evasion
Exercise price. *See* Stock apprecia-
    tion rights, *and* Stock options

F

Foreign content
    inside RRSP, 125
    portfolio in general, 181
Foreign corporation. *See*
    Incorporation
Foreign tax credit. *See* Credits
Futures contracts. *See* Investments

G

General anti-avoidance rule, 12
Gifts from employer
    non-taxable benefit, 39
Group plans
    non-taxable benefit, 39

H

Health taxes. *See* Provincial payroll
    taxes
Home Buyers' Plan. *See* Registered
    Retirement Savings Plans
Home office. *See* Deductions

I

Immigrating to Canada, 202
Income versus capital, 32
Income War Tax Act, 1
Incorporation
    Canadian controlled private cor-
        poration, 210
    corporation defined, 163
    deferring taxable income, 71
    foreign corporation, 75, 201
    investment tax credits, and, 160
    splitting taxable income, 58, 59
    tax advice, 10
Individual Pension Plans, 66
Individual Retirement Account, 114
Inflation, 175
Inheritance
    annuity payments, 87
    invest properly, 55
    non-resident, from, 202
    RRSP funds, 114
    tax advice, 11
Insurance
    Canada deposit insurance, 129
    covering taxes at death, 11
    deductible expense, 154, 155
    exempt policies, 66, 86, 206
    non-taxable benefit, 39
    policies as RRSP investment,
        110

term policies, 203, 206
whole-life policies, 206
Interest costs. *See* Deductions
Interest income
    annual accrual rule, 68, 199
    annuity, from, 67, 87. 204
    inside RRSP, 128
    instalment sales, on, 75, 88
    investments giving rise to, 174
    mutual funds, from, 31
    three-year accrual rule, 68
    versus other income, 78
Interest subsidy
    non-taxable benefit, 39
Investment amnesia, 81
Investment tax credits. *See* Credits
Investments
    classes of, 174
    diversification, 180, 181
    equity, 174
    fixed-income, 174
    futures contracts, 208
    market timing, 178
    money market, 174
    speculation, 178
    strategic investment, 178

L

Labour-Sponsored Venture Capital
    Corporations, 195
Lease costs. *See* Deductions
Leave of absence, 65
Legal costs. *See* Deductions
Life Income Funds, 131
Limited partnerships, 35, 47, 99,
    163, 191
Liquidity, 176
Loans
    between corporations, 58
    convert to shares, 85
    employees, to, 42
    fees deductible, 23
    Revenue Canada, from, 10
    Revenue Canada, to, 10
    RRSP contributions, for, 104

shareholder, to, 44, 73
small business, to, 26
splitting taxable income, 46
tax advice, 10
Locked-in RRSPs. *See* Registered
    Retirement Savings Plans
Loopholes, 6
Losses
    allowable business investment
        loss, 26, 211
    calculating earned income, 99
    capital losses, 26, 30, 32, 53,
        158, 190
    choosing a year end, 165
    commodity straddle, from, 208
    limited partnership, from, 191,
        192, 194
    non-capital, 158
    partnership, from, 163
    rental losses, 100
    sale of home, on, 38
    self-employment, from, 32, 34,
        100, 151, 158
    superficial losses, 30, 53
    transfer to spouse, 53

M

Maintenance payments, 57
Marginal tax rate. *See* Tax rates
Meals
    deductible, 156
    non-taxable benefit, 38
Medical expenses. *See* Credits
Membership fees
    deduction for employees, 20
    non-taxable benefit, 38
Mortgage
    interest deductible, 20, 154
    interest subsidy, 39
    RRSP funds to invest in your
        own, 139
    versus RRSP, 107
Mortgage subsidy
    non-taxable benefit, 37
Moving expenses. *See* Deductions

Musical instruments, 20
Mutual funds
    converting taxable income, 79, 82
    deferring income from, 69
    disposing of, 31
    distributions, 31
    exempt gains balance, 190
    inside RRSP, 109, 128
    limited partnership, 191, 193
    switching, 10, 31, 69
    timing of purchase, 187

N

Net capital loss. *See* Capital losses
Non-qualified investments. *See*
    Registered Retirement Savings
    Plans
Non-recourse debt, 192
Non-taxable benefits. *See* Benefits
Notice of assessment, 11, 36, 98
Notice of objection, 11, 20, 33, 36

O

Offshore tax planning, 75, 200

P

Partnerships, 58, 163
Penalties
    evasion, for, 5
    non-qualified RRSP investments,
        for. *See* Registered Retirement
        Savings Plans
Pension adjustment. *See* Registered
    Retirement Savings Plans
Personal tax credits. *See* Credits
Phantom stock plans, 28
Pillars of tax planning
    converting taxable income, 77
    deferring taxable income, 61
    reducing taxable income, 17
    splitting taxable income, 45
    summarized, 2

Preferred shares
    references to, 58, 77, 79, 80, 82,
        85, 197
    tax-deferred, 70, 198
Principal residence, 50, 84, 154
Private health plan
    non-taxable benefit, 39
Profit
    reasonable expectation of, 151
Proprietorship, 162
Provincial payroll taxes. *See* Tax
    payments

Q

Qualified investments. *See* Non-
    qualified investments

R

Recreational facilities
    non-taxable benefit, 38
Reducing taxable income. *See* Pillars
    of tax planning
Refund of premiums. *See* Registered
    Retirement Savings Plans
Registered Education Savings Plans,
    56, 63
Registered Pension Plans, 63, 111
Registered Retirement Income
    Funds, 130
Registered Retirement Savings Plans
    administration fees, 97
    advantages, 94, 95
    borrowing to contribute, 104
    contribution limits, 98, 100, 101
    contribution room, unused, 104
    contributions, 101, 102
    contributions in-kind, 109
    creditors, and, 96
    deductions, claiming, 106
    deferring taxable income, 63
    earned income, 99
    foreign content, 125
    home buyers' plan, 134
    inherited funds, 114

leaving Canada. *See* Emigrating
   from Canada
locked-in plans, 112
marriage break-up, 117
maturing options, 130
mortgage versus RRSP, 107
mortgage, investing in your
   own, 139
non-qualified investments, 124
over-contributions, 106
penalties, 124
pension adjustment, 64, 99
refund of premiums, 115
rollovers, 110-117
self-directed plans, 123
spousal plans
   contributions, 118, 120-122
   references to, 56
   withdrawals, 119
swapping investments with, 83
vehicle, as a, 93
withdrawals, 132, 137, 138
Reimbursements
   non-taxable benefit, 38
Relocation expenses
   non-taxable benefit, 38
Rent. *See* Deductions, and Credits
Reserves
   capital gains, 69
   income, 74
Residency, 143
Retirement Compensation
   Arrangement, 64
Retiring allowance, 65, 110
Rights
   most important right, 1
   other taxpayer rights, 3
Risk
   inflation, 175
   liquidity, 176
   market, 176
   types of, 175
Rules of thumb, 10

S

Sabbatical, 65
Salaries. *See* Deductions
Salary Deferral Arrangement, 65
Salesperson. *See* Deductions
Self-directed RRSPs. *See* Registered
   Retirement Savings Plans
Self-employment
   becoming self-employed, 147
   consulting, 149
   part-time, 34, 151
   tax shelter, as a, 148
Self-employment losses. *See* Losses
Separation, 10
Shareholder loans. *See* Loans
Splitting taxable income. *See* Pillars
   of tax planning
Stock appreciation rights, 28
Stock options, 26
Superficial loss rules. *See* Losses
Supplies. *See* Deductions

T

Tax avoidance, 6
Tax evasion, 5
Tax payments
   Canada pension plan contribu-
      tions, 166
   deferring payments, 10, 61
   instalments, 168
   provincial payroll taxes, 167
   unemployment insurance premi-
      ums, 166
Tax rates
   effective tax rate, 7
   marginal tax rate, 6
Tax shelters. *See* Limited partner-
   ships, *and* Self-employment
Taxable benefits. *See* Benefits
Tax-deferred preferred shares. *See*
   Preferred shares
Termination allowance, 110
Three-year accrual rule. *See* Interest
   income
Time value of money, 9

Transportation
  non-taxable benefit, 38
Travel costs
  deductible. See Deductions
  non-taxable benefit, 39

U
Unclaimed capital cost, 153
Unemployment insurance, 166
Uniforms
  non-taxable benefit, 38

W
Wages. *See* Salaries
Wills, 10

Y
Year end
  choosing one, 71, 164

Notes